S0-BYV-234

One
Tear
at a Time

Thank you
for your support!

Andrea
2018

One *Tear* at a Time

ANDREA REID
• • • • • • • • • • • • • •
A Mother's Journey with Raising Autistic Twins

TATE PUBLISHING
AND ENTERPRISES, LLC

One Tear at a Time
Copyright © 2013 by Andrea Reid. All rights reserved.

No part of this publication may be reproduced, stored in a retrieval system or transmitted in any way by any means, electronic, mechanical, photocopy, recording or otherwise without the prior permission of the author except as provided by USA copyright law.

This book is designed to provide accurate and authoritative information with regard to the subject matter covered. This information is given with the understanding that neither the author nor Tate Publishing, LLC is engaged in rendering legal, professional advice. Since the details of your situation are fact dependent, you should additionally seek the services of a competent professional.

The opinions expressed by the author are not necessarily those of Tate Publishing, LLC.

Published by Tate Publishing & Enterprises, LLC
127 E. Trade Center Terrace | Mustang, Oklahoma 73064 USA
1.888.361.9473 | www.tatepublishing.com

Tate Publishing is committed to excellence in the publishing industry. The company reflects the philosophy established by the founders, based on Psalm 68:11,
"The Lord gave the word and great was the company of those who published it."

Book design copyright © 2013 by Tate Publishing, LLC. All rights reserved.
Cover design by Jan Sunday Quilaquil
Interior design by Mary Jean Archival

Published in the United States of America

ISBN: 978-1-62563-831-1
1. Family & Relationships / Autism Spectrum Disorders
2. Family & Relationships / Parenting / General
13.04.25

I dedicate this book to my twins
Anthony and Andre.

I love you both very much.

Special Thank You

I'd like to say thanks to everyone who prayed for me, shared kind words of encouragement, and/or gave a helping hand. Your kind deeds will never be forgotten.

A special thank you to my mom and dad,
Rev. Burnell Reid Sr. and Mrs. Betty Reid,
for all their love and support in every way.
Without my parent's support, this
would not have been possible.

Thank you to my loved ones,
Robert
Jamel
Burnell Jr.
Donnell
Lonnell

Also thank you to my church families,

Refuge Tabernacle Church of God
in Christ, Syracuse, New York
Refreshing Spring Church of God in
Christ, Riverdale, Maryland

God bless you all.

A Word to the Reader

This book is designed to enhance your knowledge and understanding of lives affected by autism and hopefully gives you a sense of compassion toward those that live daily with this disability.

Every day, more and more children are being diagnosed with autism. My life has been severely affected by autism, which inspired me to share my story with you. As you read this book, please read it not with sadness but with hope for a brighter future and hope for a possible cure.

I truly believe that God didn't bring me to this situation if He didn't plan to bring me through it.

Be blessed!

Contents

The Diagnosis

On a cold wintery afternoon sometime during March 2005, I was handed a diagnosis that would change my life forever. I realized that life comes with its ups and downs, its good days and bad days, but no matter what, no life lesson could prepare me for the journey I was about to take.

As a child and straight up through adulthood, I dreamed of how life was going to be for me. My dreams included love, marriage, and family. As an adult, I strived diligently to make a good life for my children and myself, yet daily life events continuously challenged my dreams, hope, and my faith.

The wintery afternoon I walked into the Medical Developmental Evaluation Center, I was expecting to receive answers as to why my three-year-old son could not talk. In my mind, this would be a quick, no-brainer, to-the-point appointment. Instead, I was handed a diagnosis that changed my life forever: autism. This doctor was supposed to tell me that my son was fine and that he was just a little behind the average child his age. I was supposed to be told that in a few months, my child would be talking just like any other child his age. I sat in that doctor's office confused and desperate for answers. *Autism*—my son has autism.

I began thinking to myself, what is autism? Did this doctor just use some fancy word to tell me in a roundabout way that my son is mentally retarded? I've never heard of autism nor did I really understand what it meant to be diagnosed with autism so naturally I had questions. There were hundreds of questions running through my mind with no answers. Is this doctor trying to tell me that Andre is not normal? I could hear the doctor's voice lingering in the background of the room as he tried to explain autism and what this meant for Andre, but honestly, I didn't hear a word he was saying. I continued to sit and listen, when suddenly, I heard the words *autism* and *brain disorder* used in the same sentence.

Actually, the doctor said to me, "Your child has a brain disorder." This is not making any sense to me. I came to this appointment because my child is three years old and cannot talk, and now I'm being told that my child has a brain disorder. I looked at the doctor and demanded that he explain to me in a way that I could better understand what he was telling me. I needed to make sure I left this appointment with no misunderstandings or doubt. He proceeded to use a different approach at explaining *autism* to me. After hearing his explanation, I still couldn't help but wonder what part of this appointment prompted this doctor to diagnose my child with autism.

Walking through the hallways of the Medical Developmental Evaluation Center, I noticed that this building resembled a regular elementary school. Instead of the main office, there was a reception area. I walked up to the main desk and gave mine and Andre's name. I told the receptionist that we had an appointment for 1:00 PM. She noted that we had arrived and told me to have a seat. The waiting area had toys that most children would have played with. Andre had no interest in these toys: he just twirled his pencils between his fingers. Approximately five minutes after we had sat down, a team of doctors, psychiatrists, and therapist entered the waiting area and greeted us. They introduced themselves one at a time. Each person tried to engage in conversation with Andre, but Andre did not respond. The psychiatrist began to explain to me what was about to happen. Each person would take Andre to a specific area and attempt to evaluate him. This doctor made it clear that my participation should be little to none. They wanted to evaluate Andre's abilities without any help from me. I was allowed to be in the same room but was asked not to help in any way. I acknowledged that I understood the procedures and agreed to them.

The first therapist prompted Andre and I to follow her down the hallway. The inside of this building really looked like an elementary school, but behind the doors was a totally different setting.

We walked into the first room, and there was a table placed in the middle with a chair placed on each side of the table. I was prompted to sit in a chair that was on the opposite side of the room away from Andre and the therapist. Andre sat in the chair for a few seconds and then got up and turned to the window. Andre stood, looking out the window while twirling his pencil between his fingers. The therapist tried unsuccessfully to get Andre to participate so that she could evaluate him. Andre was not interested at all. On this table were boards and blocks. The therapist was trying to get Andre to place the square block into the square hole, the round block into the round role, and the triangle block into the triangle hole; but Andre had no interest. After ten minutes of trying to get Andre to participate, the therapist looked at me and asked if I could help get Andre to at least sit down at the table.

I replied, "I was told that I was not to offer any help." So the therapist picked up her chair and one of the boards and went over to the window where Andre was standing. She tried again but again was unsuccessful. I felt that this therapist was getting frustrated because she could not get any participation from Andre whatsoever. Twenty minutes had gone by, and the next therapist had come into the room. It was time to move to the next stage of this evaluation.

We again walked down the hallway of this building. There were three levels to this building. We walked up to a flight of stairs and the therapist explained to me that she was looking to see how many steps could Andre walk up without assistance. In this procedure, Andre was more cooperative. Andre grabbed the stair rail and walked up the entire set of stairs without any assistance. The therapist walked close behind him just in case he needed help. When they got to the top of the stairs, the therapist told Andre to turn around and walk back down the stairs. Andre had no problem walking down the stairs alone, but halfway down the stairs, he lost his balance, and the therapist had to help him regain his balance, and he continued on his own down the stairs.

We again walked down the hallway, and at the end of the hallway was a gymnasium. We walk in, and the therapist wanted to see if Andre could run, hop, jump, and skip on his own. Again, Andre would not participate. He would only walk the trail that was there for him to run, jump, hop, and skip on. The therapist looked at me and asked if I had ever seen Andre do any of these things. I replied that he runs all the time, and I have seen him jump a few time. But I had not seen him skip or hop on one foot or on both feet.

At this point, we walked down the hallway to another room. In this room, there was a sliding board, a tire swing, a trampoline, and various other toys. The therapist allowed Andre to engage with the different activities on his own. Andre ran over to the tire swing and sat there until the next person came to take us to the next step in this evaluation process.

This time, a medical doctor came to get us. We walked down the hallway into another door. Behind this door, the room resembled a doctor's medical examination room. This doctor checked Andre from head to toe. His did what is known as a head-to-toe assessment. He checked Andre's weight and height as well. After the completed head-to-toe assessment, we again walked down the hallway into yet another room. The psychiatrist that explained the procedure in the beginning was sitting in this room, waiting for us. Everyone that had seen Andre had given a report to this psychiatrist, reporting their finding and their recommendation. It was at this moment I was handed the diagnosis of autism.

It's my turn to talk and ask questions. I wanted to know if there was a pill or a surgery that could cure this thing called autism. How is this going to affect my son's life? Where do I go for help? What can I do to help my son? What's going to happen next? I kept thinking that my child is just a little behind other children his age; he's going to be fine. How does a brain disorder fit into this thing called autism? I stood up to leave the doctor's office; he filled my hands with pamphlets and brochures and felt compelled to tell me that there are support groups that could help me with this. He gave me websites to search and visit and told me to go to the library and read up on autism. He also told me to feel free to call his office at any time with any and all questions I may have. He advised me to talk with my pediatrician as well.

As I walked to my car holding my son's hand, I was still confused and not 100 percent sure about autism. One could say that I was perhaps in a state of denial. In my mind, I was not going to allow myself to accept that my son was mentally retarded. Although mental retardation was not the diagnosis given and because I knew very little about autism, it just seemed right to blame *mental retardation*.

I needed to talk to someone who could help me understand what I had just been told. As I opened the door to my car, I felt that denial had found a home in my mind and in my heart. Sitting in the driver seat of my car, I began to think, *This can't be right. Autism, a brain disorder, mental retardation—this couldn't be what's wrong with my son. Look at my son. He looks normal, he just can't talk, there is no way he has a brain disorder.*

Exactly one week later, I had another appointment at the same place for my second three-year-old twin, Anthony. I hesitated to go to this appointment because of what I was told the last time I was here. Why should I go back to the same place and see the same doctor and let him tell me more nonsense this time about Anthony and allow him to upset me once again? I knew in my heart that the results for Anthony's would be the same, or maybe even worst. But per the advice of family members, I kept the appointment.

I walked through the doors of the Medical Developmental Evaluation Center again, not happy to be there at all. I walked into the reception area and gave my name and Anthony's name. I told the receptionist that we had an appointment for 1:30 PM. She noted that we had arrived and told me to have a seat. Just like Andre, Anthony had no interest in the toys in the waiting area. The evaluation team came into the waiting area and acknowledged that they remembered me from Andre and then proceeded to introduce themselves to Anthony. Being that Anthony was totally nonverbal, there was no response. The psychiatrist again explained to me what was about to happen. Each person would take Anthony to a specific area and attempt to evaluate him. Again, it was made very clear that in order to receive an accurate evaluation, my participation should be little to none. I acknowledged that I understood, and I agreed to the procedures.

The first therapist prompted Anthony and I to follow her down the hallway. We walked into the first room and the same table setting was placed in the middle of the room with a chair placed on each side of the table. I knew without being told what I could and could not do. Anthony sat in the chair and the therapist began to try to get Anthony to participate. At first, Anthony touched each block as the therapist placed them in front of him. After the third block, Anthony pushed the blocks away from him. He also pushed the boards away from him. The therapist tried to take his string from him, thinking she could get Anthony to participate more if he wasn't holding on to that string. Well, Anthony became very upset. He stood up and knocked over his chair and began to cry and push everything off the table. The therapist looked at me and asked me to help. I wanted to say, "I was told that I was not to offer any help," but I saw how upset my child had become, so I told the therapist that the only way to calm Anthony down was to give him back his string. She replied that his string was a total distraction. In my mind, I was thinking, *You are the professional, so you need to find another way to evaluate Anthony while allowing him to keep his string.*

Unfortunately, the therapist was unsuccessful in getting Anthony to participate without his string, and Anthony had become so frustrated that even after giving him back his string, he would not participate. It was time for the next therapist to take over. The first therapist explained that Anthony was a little upset. I'm guessing she was giving her co-worker a heads-up.

We walked down the hallway to the set of stairs. Again, the object was to observe Anthony to see how many steps he could walk up without assistance. Anthony did cooperate and with no problems walked up the stairs holding on the stair rail. The therapist walked close behind him just in case he needed help. When they got to the top of the stairs, the therapist told Anthony to turn around and walk back down the stairs. Anthony would not turn around; in fact, Anthony started leaning backward over the stairs as if he was going to allow his body to fall backward down the stairs. The therapist was holding a clipboard, which I assume she was using to take notes on. As I stood at the bottom of the stairs, I saw the clipboard go sailing through the air, and the therapist reached out to Anthony in fear. As she reached for Anthony, he turned around, grabbed the stair rail, and started walking down the stairs. When they both reached the bottom of the stairs, she looked at me and said that her heart skipped a few beats. She thought Anthony was going to fall down the stairs. I told her that Anthony always plays on the stairs at home. I also said that Anthony is a daredevil; he likes to try things most children his age wouldn't try, but he would never do anything that would cause him pain. Anthony knows that falling down the stairs would cause him pain, so he's very cautious when playing on the stairs. I told the therapist that I was not sure why Anthony chose to scare her like that, but I knew that he was not going to hurt himself.

We proceeded to walk down the hallway to the gymnasium. We walk in, and the therapist prompted Anthony to run, hop, jump, and skip. Anthony ran down the trail but only with the therapist holding his hand. He also jumped on two feet, but again, only with the therapist holding his hand. He would not hop or skip with or without assistance. The therapist asked if I had ever seen Anthony hop or skip on his own or with assistance. I replied that I have seen him run, climb, and jump; but I don't remember seeing him hop or skip.

Now it was time to go to the room with the sliding board, a tire swing, and the trampoline. The therapist allowed Anthony to engage with the different activities on his own. There was also a set of toy steps. Anthony ran over to steps, walked up and down the stairs a few times, then went over to the tire swing. He sat on the swing until it was time to visit with the medical doctor. We walked into the examination room, and the doctor began to exam Anthony.

Unfortunately, Anthony would not cooperate. During the head-to-toe assessment, Anthony would not sit still. The doctor even had to guess Anthony's weight and height because he just would not stand still long enough to get an accurate measurement. After the examination, we walked down the hallway into the room where the psychiatrist was waiting for us. He had received everyone's report, their finding, and their recommendation. Again, another diagnosis of autism, but this time, this child was diagnosed as severely autistic.

Just as I expected, the results for Anthony were worse. He was diagnosed severely autistic, and I was told that Anthony would need assistance and supervision throughout his life. The doctor told me that Anthony would not be able to live a normal life in society without proper assistance. I didn't have any questions with this appointment. My heart was broken, and I felt like I had been handed a death sentence for my child. This time, when I left the medical center, I was in tears. As I stood up to walk toward the exit, the tears started to flow one tear at a time.

The Explanation

I began to do research because I wanted to prove that the doctor was wrong about my boys. My children are fine. They are just a little delayed verbally. I went to the library and looked up autism. I found several books and quite a few websites that offered a variety of definitions about autism. I sat for hours reading and surfing the web. While reading, I came across an article that explained how to recognize the signs and symptoms of autism. I decided to write down the symptoms that I thought applied to my boys. On a blank sheet of paper, I wrote both boys' names. Every symptom that I read about that I felt applied to Anthony, I wrote under his name. I did the same for Andre. I was surprised at how many symptoms applied to both of my boys.

One definition I got from the web stated that

> Autism is a disorder of neural development characterized by impaired social interaction and communication, and by restricted and repetitive behavior. These signs all begin before a child is three years old. Autism affects information processing in the brain by altering how nerve cells and their synapses connect and organize; how this occurs is not well understood. It is one of three recognized disorders in the

autism spectrum (ASDs), the other two being Asperger Syndrome, which lacks delays in cognitive development and language, and Pervasive Developmental Disorder-Not Otherwise Specified (commonly abbreviated as PDD-NOS), which is diagnosed when the full set of criteria for autism or Asperger syndrome are not met.

Autism has a strong genetic basis, although the genetics of autism are complex, and it is unclear whether ASD is explained more by rare mutations, or by rare combinations of common genetic variants. In rare cases, autism is strongly associated with agents that cause birth defects. Controversies surround other proposed environmental causes, such as heavy metals, pesticides or childhood vaccines; the vaccine hypotheses are biologically implausible and lack convincing scientific evidence. The prevalence of autism is about 1–2 per 1,000 people; the prevalence of ASD is about 6 per 1,000, affecting about four times as many males as females. The number of people diagnosed with autism has increased dramatically since the 1980s, partly due to changes in diagnostic practice; the question of whether actual prevalence has increased is unresolved

Parents usually notice signs of Autism in the first two years of their child's life. The signs usually develop gradually, but some autistic children first develop more normally and then regress. Although early behavioral or cognitive intervention can help autistic children gain self-care, social, and communication skills, there is no known cure. Not many children with autism live independently after reaching adulthood, though some become successful. An autistic culture has developed, with some individuals seeking a cure and others believing autism should be tolerated as a difference and not treated as a disorder.

Diagnosis is based on behavior, not cause or mechanism. Autism is defined when exhibiting at least six symptoms total, including at least two symptoms of qualitative impairment in social interaction, at least one symptom of qualitative impairment in communication, and at least one symptom of restricted and repetitive behavior. Sample symptoms include lack of social or emotional reciprocity, stereotyped and repetitive use of language or idiosyncratic language, and persistent preoccupation with parts of objects. Onset must be prior to age three years, with delays or abnormal functioning in either social interaction, language as used in social communication, or symbolic or imaginative play.[1]

Below is a diagram of the brain that became of great interest to me. It explains how Autism affects the amygdala, cerebellum, and many other parts of the brain. (http://en.wikipedia. org/wiki/Autism, 2011)

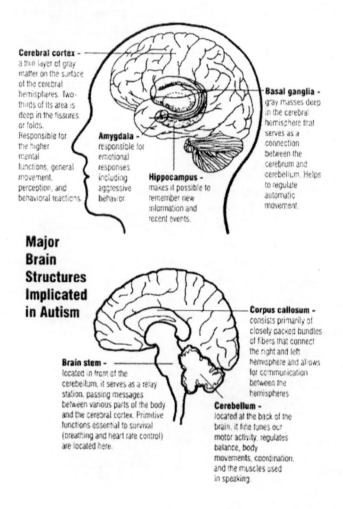

Cerebral cortex - a thin layer of gray matter on the surface of the cerebral hemispheres. Two-thirds of its area is deep in the fissures or folds. Responsible for the higher mental functions, general movement, perception, and behavioral reactions.

Amygdala - responsible for emotional responses, including aggressive behavior

Hippocampus - makes it possible to remember new information and recent events.

Basal ganglia - gray masses deep in the cerebral hemisphere that serves as a connection between the cerebrum and cerebellum. Helps to regulate automatic movement.

Major Brain Structures Implicated in Autism

Corpus callosum - consists primarily of closely packed bundles of fibers that connect the right and left hemisphere and allows for communication between the hemispheres

Brain stem - located in front of the cerebellum, it serves as a relay station, passing messages between various parts of the body and the cerebral cortex. Primitive functions essential to survival (breathing and heart rate control) are located here.

Cerebellum - located at the back of the brain, it fine tunes our motor activity, regulates balance, body movements, coordination, and the muscles used in speaking.

28

One of the signs and symptoms I recognized in my boys was how socially they fail to respond to their name, which was common for children with autism. Some children have poor eye contact, they appear not to hear you at times, some resist cuddling and holding, and appear unaware of others' feelings and seem to prefer playing alone. As for communication, they start talking later than age two, lose their previously acquired ability to say words or sentences, don't make eye contact when making requests, speak with an abnormal tone or rhythm such as a robotlike speech, can't start a conversation or keep one going, and they may repeat words or phrases verbatim but do not really understand how to use them.

Behaviorally, children with autism perform repetitive movements such as rocking, spinning, or hand flapping. They develop specific routines and become disturbed at the slightest change in their routine. They move constantly and may be fascinated by parts of an object such as the spinning wheels of a toy car. They may be unusually sensitive to light, sound, and touch yet oblivious to pain.

As I continued to read, I began to understand more about autism. I had to admit that after reading several websites and books and recognizing the signs and symptoms in both of my boys, it was enough to convince me to finally accept their diagnosis. My heart was heavy as I left the library. I began to wonder how this happened and why.

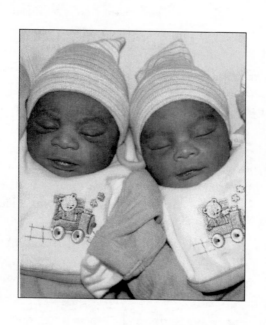

The Birth

During the year 1995, I thought life was great. I was educated, had a good job, and had just married a good man. It didn't take long before the many pressures of life started to close in on me and caused my life to start falling apart.

On May 16, 2002, I gave birth to a beautiful set of twin boys. As I listened to them cry for the very first time and looked in their little faces, a sense of joy filled my heart. As I was rolled out of the delivery room with a child in each arm, I thanked God for such a miracle, a wonder blessing—two babies at once. My husband, whom I'll call Adam, followed closely, videotaping the entire event.

Giving birth to twins was a life-changing event. It was going to be an adjustment to our lives, but we were ready. Adam and I had put our heads together and came up with what we thought was the perfect game plan to raise our twins and be the best parents ever. It wasn't long before reality settled in. Caring for twins was a lot tougher than we thought. There were many tears shed as well as several sleepless nights. Everything was doubled: double the diaper changing, double the laundry, double the feedings, but we hung in there and made it work.

As my maternity leave came to an end, we had to prepare for my return to work. At this point, we had to really kick our support system into full force because without each other, we knew that our mission couldn't be done.

Two years after the twins were born, Adam and I became legally separated. Being married came with its difficult moments, and we allowed these moments to interfere in our lives. Soon the pressures of life had taken over, which brought about an end to this marriage. Our separation had nothing to do with autism. Shortly after the separation, five months to be exact, we became divorced, and within weeks after the divorce, my twins were diagnosed with autism. I was an emotional wreck. I'm now a single parent who had to deal with autism alone. Going through a divorce was tough, but having to deal with autism alone was tougher. Daily, I watched things in my life fall apart piece by piece until I eventually moved out of my world of happiness and into a world of divorce, single parenting, and autism. This was not my dream life; this was more like a nightmare. Tears began to flow, one tear at a time.

I began to think about my life, going back to my childhood. I was born and raised in a two-parent family, a family full of love. I am the eldest of four siblings and the only girl. My parents provided a good life for us.

Many would say that because I was the only girl, I was spoiled. I agreed to a certain degree, but my parents provided a life for me that inspired me to dream big.

My parents were very active in our lives. There was never a time that we were hungry, homeless, or without needs or wants. My parents made sure of that.

My family is very spiritual and religious. I was raised in the Pentecostal religion, and we attended church services on a regular basis. My brothers and I were raised to believe in God and to love and worship God. My dad, Rev. Burnell Reid Sr., became a pastor, and my mom, Mrs. Betty Reid, became a missionary in the church.

My dad is a very unique man. He's kind, loving, understanding, and compassionate towards everyone. He loves my mom very much, and he took pride in keeping our family together under one roof. He was always very active in our lives. Quality time was very important to my dad.

As a girl, my dad taught me a lot. What I remember the most is how my dad would take me bike riding and spend time teaching me basketball. As a teenager, my dad would wake me up at the break of dawn to teach me how to drive. Some mornings while out driving, he would take me to breakfast or just grab some donuts and a cup of hot chocolate. I had what most children only dream of, a father who cared and showed it daily.

My mom was the strict parent. Although she loved us very much, she said what she meant and meant what she said. Mom made sure our chores and homework were done. Mom taught us about hygiene, to respect ourselves and others, what good manners meant, and she constantly reminded us of the importance of education. My mom taught me the things I would need to know to survive as a lady in life. Just like my dad, my mom cared a great deal about our family. Together, my parents provided what was to me the perfect family.

When I found out I was pregnant with my twins, my mom began to pray for them. She said that God had dropped in her spirit to pray for a blood transfusion for my twins. She was not really sure why God had placed this desire to pray for the twins on her heart, but she started praying and never stopped. I went into premature labor about twenty-six weeks into the pregnancy. I thought, *This is why God wanted my mom to pray*. Because of the premature labor, I was hospitalized for almost the remainder of my pregnancy. My mom began to pray even more. Before going into premature labor, I had developed gestational diabetes.

While in the hospital, I was hooked up to all sorts of machines and was given drugs daily to help stabilize my condition. I was given magnesium sulfate, to help stop or even slow down my contractions; steroids, corticosteriods, to speed up lung development in the twins; drugs to stabilize my blood pressure; and insulin to stabilize my blood glucose levels. I also had consultation with the Newborn Intensive Care Unit doctor just in case the attempts to stop premature labor failed, and my babies, for whatever reason, needed help to survive. The entire time, my mom continued to pray.

Although I was hospitalized and injected with different medications, my twins were born seven weeks early. They were fine, two perfect bundles of joy. They had two eyes, a nose, a mouth, ten fingers and toes; and they were able to breathe on their own. I thought to myself, "Mom can stop praying now, the babies are fine."

All the ups and downs that life presented me, nothing I have experienced could have prepared me for autism.

Single Parenting

As I continued to research autism and talk with doctors and therapists, my understanding became more and more clear about what was happening with my boys. I understood that I had a long journey ahead of me. I had to accept the fact that this journey was not going to be easy. Most importantly, I learned how expensive it was going to be. The financial aspect of this entire ordeal scared me the most. Although I had a good job and was receiving child support, I knew it was still going to be hard financially. My boys were going to need special services that could become very expensive. I'm a single parent with two children diagnosed with autism, and now I have to add finances to my already overloaded plate. I'm starting to feel like I'm being punished for whatever reason. The tears began to flow, one tear at a time.

I began to cry every night as reality began to settle in. I felt as if someone had snatched my heart out of my chest and left me alone to die. I felt as if the world was against me, and happiness could no longer be mine. I began to pray and ask God for strength. I prayed that God would increase my faith and help me make it through this trial. But no matter how much I prayed, the pain of reality lingered on, refusing to go away.

As time went on, I found myself exhausted daily. I was running from doctor to doctor, therapist to therapist, school to school, and meeting to meeting. I had become my children's sole provider both physically and emotionally, and it was starting to take an effect on me.

Shortly after their diagnoses, I was able to get the boys into a preschool program that would provide them with some of the special services they needed. This program provided speech, occupational and physical therapy, and an opportunity for the boys to be around other children their age. This program was considered to be what is called an inclusive program, which meant that the boys would be allowed in classrooms with other children that had no disability at all as well as other children with autism.

At the end of most days, I was so exhausted that when I laid my head on my pillow at night, I basically passed out from exhaustion. I was working a full-time job, raising three children (Jamel, Anthony, and Andre), two of which were autistic, and I was trying to remain active in my spiritual church life.

At this point in my life, I thought things could not get any worse. I was wrong. One morning, I received a phone call from school, the pre-k program where the boys attended. Anthony had suddenly developed uncontrollable temper tantrums. These outbreaks were unexplained, severe, and somewhat violent. After the teachers had struggle with him for over twenty minutes and with no success, the director of the program called me at work and said that I needed to come and get Anthony.

This posed no problem with my job, at first. I was able to leave and bring Anthony home. To my surprise, he calmed right down and was fine for the rest of the day.

The next day, I got the boys up and ready for school. We were off to a good start. Anthony was calm and in a good mood, so the boys got on the bus and headed off to pre-k. Minutes before noon that day, I received another call from the school. Anthony again was having a breakdown that was unexplained, uncontrollable, and violent. My employer was not happy about me having to leave again, but I had no choice.

When I arrived in the school, the teachers had placed Anthony in a room away from the other students where he was being supervised by his occupational therapist. As I walked into the room, Anthony was sitting in a chair. His eyes were red and swollen. I could tell that he had been crying, but he didn't seem to be uncontrollable or violent. When he saw me walk through the door, he stood up and ran toward me, grabbed my hand, and petitioned for us to leave. The therapist said, "We'll try again tomorrow." As I walked to the car hand in hand with Anthony, I was confused. Anthony seemed just fine. The way the director described Anthony's behavior to me over the phone, I expected to see more than just red, swollen eyes. He sat in his car seat just as calmed and relaxed as any child. I was missing time off my job, and I really didn't understand why. Anthony seemed fine to me.

I sent the boys to school again the next day. I was at work for three hours and received another call from the pre-k program. This time, I was told that Anthony was completely uncontrollable and not only violent toward himself but also to others around him. I was told that he was biting, pulling hair, and scratching. One of the teachers tried to restrain him and was thrown to the ground. When I arrived at the school, this time, Anthony was still in his classroom. As I walked through the door, I stood frozen in my steps as I witnessed Anthony having a meltdown. I was shocked. I watched the teachers unsuccessfully gain control. I stood and witnessed a teacher fall to the ground as she tried to restrain Anthony. I stood in the doorway, unable to move with tears rolling down my cheeks. I could not believe that this was my child in such a rage. Who is this person? What is going on with my child? Why is he acting like this? True confusion cluttered my mind as I stood and witnessed this rage. I walked over toward Anthony with a purpose of gaining control. When Anthony saw me, he continued crying, but the lashing out at others stopped. Before I left the school, I was told that Anthony could not return until the tantrums were under control. I was advised to take him to his pediatrician.

Once in the car, Anthony began to calm down. I sat in the parking lot of the school and called the doctor immediately using my cell phone. I needed a same day appointment. It was imperative that Anthony be able to return to school as soon as possible, preferably the next day, because I had to get back to work. I was able to get a doctor's appointment for that same day. The nurse told me to bring Anthony in right away. I could barely drive because tears had consumed my eyes.

We arrived at the doctor's office and patiently sat in the waiting area. Suddenly, Anthony began to have another tantrum. Now it's my turn to wrestle with him. I had to gain control of this tantrum all by myself. Sitting in that waiting area wrestling with Anthony, I became embarrassed. I tried everything to calm him down, but nothing was working. I wanted to cry, but I couldn't waste my energy on tears. I needed all my strength to continue to wrestle with Anthony. People began to stare. The nurse finally came to help. She too was unsuccessful, so she helped me take Anthony into an examination room where we had more privacy as we waited for the doctor.

When the doctor walked into the room, I was still wrestling with Anthony. He was just not going to calm down. The doctor proceeded to help me. As we both wrestled with Anthony, somehow, Anthony's foot became free, and he kicked the doctor. I could see pain all in the doctor's eyes. After several minutes of being unsuccessful in gaining control with Anthony, he finally began to calm down. His eyes were red, like fire, and he was panting hard as if he couldn't catch his breath. I could see his little heart beating through his shirt.

The doctor proceeded to ask me questions regarding the tantrums. He wanted to know when Anthony started behaving like this and what he is usually doing when the tantrums start. This was all new to me. I couldn't really answer the doctor's questions because these tantrums usually started at school. I had never witness any such tantrum at home. Well, I left the doctor's office with three prescriptions and a brief explanation of each drug and the possible adverse effects. This doctor did warn me that each prescription could have an addictive adverse effect. As I approached the front desk to pay my co-pay, I noticed that the doctor had written a diagnosis of "Global Retardation" on Anthony's exam form.

This was a little too much for me to handle. I'm missing time off my job, I'm exhausted from wrestling with Anthony, and now, the pediatrician has labeled my son as retarded.

It was obvious that I was not going to be able to go back to work the next day. I was afraid of what my boss was going to say, but thank God I found out that I was protected under the Family Medical Leave Act (FMLA); therefore, I was able to take a few days off.

First thing's first, I needed to find out what *global retardation* meant and why the pediatrician placed this label on my son. The only information I could find was a definition about retardation. I read that significantly impaired cognitive functioning and deficits in two or more adaptive behaviors characterize *mental retardation*. So now am I suppose to believe that my son is mentally retarded because of these tantrums? I am more confused now than ever and completely unwilling to accept this diagnosis.

While off from work, I had made up my mind that I was going to do whatever I had to do to make sure that Anthony was okay and able to return to school without any complications or interference. The last thing I wanted was to go back to work and receive another call, asking me to remove Anthony from school again.

As I sat home during my days off, I kept thinking on the diagnosis the doctor had handed Anthony of global retardation. It continued to weigh very heavy on my mind. I also wanted to know more about the drugs he prescribed for Anthony. I needed to know about the possible adverse effects they would have on my son. One of the drugs prescribed was Ritalin, and the adverse effects that concerned me were the suppression of growth and possible addiction. I also read that Ritalin should not be given to children under the age of six. This drug was intended to help children with hyperactive and impulsive behavior. After reading this and the fact that my son was only four years old, I refused to give him this or any medication. I called the doctor's office and explained to the nurse how I felt and why I refuse to give the meds. The nurse informed the doctor of my decision and told me that the doctor was not happy with my decision. At this point, I was told that if I didn't give Anthony these drugs, he could not return to school, and I could possibly be reported for neglect. The doctor had reportedly given me the medical answer to the violent outbreaks that my son was experiencing by prescribing drugs, and my refusal to administer the drugs was a form of neglect.

I was more anxious now than ever before to help my son. I needed to find a way to help without putting these drugs into his body. I was torn. I needed Anthony back in school, but I did not want to give my child these drugs. I made a few phone calls. I spoke with a therapist, Anthony's teachers, a psychologist, a nurse, and my family and friends seeking advice and possibly an answer. The responses I received did not help much; I still did not want to give my son these drugs. I felt in my heart that there had to be a better solution. I spent days and hours researching and surfing the web, hoping to find a solution I could be satisfied with.

As the days rolled by, I couldn't find anything to help Anthony, but I refused to give up. One day, a friend called and said she had found an herbal medicine that was equivalent to Ritalin without the adverse addictive effects. I researched this herbal remedy and liked the results I found. I immediately ran to the organic health store where I was able to speak with a licensed nutritionist. I began to explain this herbal medicine and asked if there was any advice she could offer. She not only gave great feedback, but the information she provided was outstanding. The longer she talked, I noticed that she was also giving me information on other herbal remedies, vitamins, and health drinks that she reassured me would help. She explained everything thoroughly and gave me pamphlets to read. She told me that she had recommended the same remedies to other autistic children, and the parents have been very pleased with the results. I purchased all that I could afford that day and immediately went home and began to give my son the medications. As I gave this herbal medicine to Anthony, I monitored him closely. An entire week had gone by, and I noticed how calm and relaxed Anthony had become. I began to thank God for placing friends in my life that cared and wanted to help. I thank God for placing that licensed nutritionist in that organic health store. She was in the right place at the right time just for me. I thank God for the peace that was in my home at that moment.

After one week of taking the herbal medications, Anthony was allowed to return to school, and I went back to work.

Special Services for Special Needs

It was that time of the year, scheduled parent-teacher conference time. Not only did I have parent-teacher conferences to attend, I also had to attend an Individualized Education Program (IEP) meeting for both boys. During the IEP meeting, I was told that both Anthony and Andre would not be able to attend kindergarten because they were not potty trained, and they both were nonverbal. So now what do I do? I was told that there were programs that could possibly help the boys with their speech. These programs provided services such as speech and language therapy and occupational therapy, which would also help with potty training. I was handed a list of agency to contact. I made call after call, and each program I called charged a tuition that I could not afford. Then I was given information on how to apply for grants and other funds to help pay the tuition for these special services. I wasn't too much surprise when the agencies I called placed me on a waiting list. Because so many children have been diagnosed with autism, and parents have been seeking financial help, available grants or funds have been depleted.

I decided to take matters into my own hands. I was going to potty train my children and help them learn to talk if it was the last thing I do. How hard could it be? My goal was to have both boys potty trained and talking before the end of the school year. I went to the store and bought two potty chairs and a bundle of training underpants and began to dedicate myself to getting the job done.

For days and even weeks, I remain faithful to potty training my boys. I was starting to get frustrated because nothing I tried was working. My plan was to make the boys sit on their potty chairs every hour on the hour. I would read books and sang songs to the boys, hoping this would inspire them to talk. I even tried making them drink a lot of fluids, but that didn't work either. The boys had no interest in using the potty or talking.

Soon it was summertime, the school year was over, and to my disappointment, neither twin was potty trained or talking. Andre starting using the potty when placed in the seated position, but he could not tell me when he needed to go because he was still nonverbal. Potty training was a lot harder than I thought it would be, mainly because the boys were nonverbal. It was near impossible to guess when they had to go; I needed them to tell me. Every day was like playing a guessing game. I tried to keep track of their bladder and bowel patterns by making a chart of every time they wet or soiled their training underwear. This didn't work either. Every day, the time they would wet or soil their training underwear would change. So I tried letting the boys walk around the house in their training underpants all day. Then I found myself mopping more than usual, and my laundry loads had tripled, but it would be worth it all if I can get these boys potty trained. I didn't mind the mopping, but all of a sudden, I found myself cleaning up poop. I was cleaning poop off the floors, off the walls, out of the carpet, off toys, and anything they touched. Anthony would have a bowel movement, and before I could get him cleaned up, he would play with what didn't fall out of his training underpants. With poop on his hands, anything he touched was left stained. Every day I found myself mopping up urine and cleaning up poop. Anthony would have poop on the bottom of his feet, on both hands, in his hair, and sometimes on his face. I would have to carry him to the bathtub to avoid tracking poop throughout the house. I would leave Anthony in the tub for twenty minutes or more to get rid of the odor. The poop accidents happened three, sometimes four, times a week. I was again becoming frustrated and feeling like I could not do this. Everything I tried was not working. I was ready to give up. Potty training the twins felt impossible. The tears begin to flow down my cheeks, one tear at a time.

Life was truly getting the best of me. I felt like I was definitely being punished. What did I do to deserve this? No matter what I try, nothing worked. I found myself crying myself to sleep almost every night. What kind of life is this? I hate my life. I'm divorced, raising twins with autism, finding myself on my hands and knees cleaning up poop, and at the end of my rope financially. I love my boys, but this thing called autism is wearing me down. I wouldn't trade my life with anyone. I can't image that anyone would want my life. At this point, I was starting to become depressed, and I was losing hope. No matter how much I prayed, things just kept getting worse. I truly hated my life, and I did not want to face my trials and tribulations any more. This particular night, before I got in bed, my eyes filled with tears. I prayed and asked God to let me fall asleep and never to wake again. I didn't want to wake up and face another day of disappointment, heartache, financial distress, and autism. I was tired and did not believe I had the strength to continue to fight. I really felt that if God would allow me to close my eyes and never open them again, all the pain would go away. No more disappointments, heartache, and most of all, no more dealing with autism. The tears ran endlessly down my cheeks. I had a pain in my stomach that was indescribable. I had truly reached the bottom. I had actually sat on the side of my bed and prayed to die.

Meningitis

I've had my share of life's ups and downs. Autism is just one of the many things I've had to deal with in this life. Some years ago, 1993 to be exact, I lost a child to a tragic case of meningitis.

It was a beautiful, sunny Saturday morning, and my two sons, Robert and Michael, went outside to play. They were enjoying a long break from school due to the Memorial Day holiday. They would run in and out of the house only to eat, drink, and use the bathroom and would race back outside to play. My youngest son, Jamel, would bounce up and down in his baby walker with excitement every time Robert and Michael would run into the house. I knew Jamel wanted to go outside, but he was still a baby, too young to go outside with his big brothers.

The sun was going down, and it was getting late, so I called for the boys to come inside for the night. We all settled down for the evening by watching television before going to bed. My baby Jamel was the first to fall asleep, and Michael fell asleep shortly while lying on the floor in front of the television. Robert woke Michael up, and they went to bed together.

On Sunday morning, we all got up and went to Sunday morning church service. On Sunday afternoon, around 1:00 PM, Michael developed a fever. When we arrived home from church, I gave him Tylenol, and he laid down and slept for most of the day. About 9:30 PM that night, he woke up and told me he was thirsty. I gave him a glass of water, and he began to shake as if he was having a seizure. I called the doctor immediately and was told to take his temperature. His temperature registered at 102 degrees. The doctor said that the shakes were probably a result of giving him cold water with such a high fever. I was instructed to give him more Tylenol and rub alcohol over his entire body. I did just as the doctor instructed me, and my son went back to bed and went to sleep. At 5:30 AM, I could hear Michael moaning very loud, so I went into his bedroom to check on him. My son had broken out in purple spots all over his body, and his temperature had spiked up to 104. My oldest brother, Burnell Jr., had stayed with me that night. I yelled out to my brother, and he came running into Michael's room. He took one look at Michael, wrapped him in a blanket, and we rushed him to the emergency room. The admitting nurse began to ask questions, trying to figure out where the purple spots came from. She tried over and over to get Michael's vital signs. His pulse rate was so weak that she was unsuccessful at getting an accurate reading. I remember the nurse calling for help. I watched her as she put on a face mask, and without saying anything, she picked up Michael and ran down the hall into an examination room with him. Minutes went by, and no one said anything to me about what was going on with my son. The doctor finally came out to talk to me and said my son was in serious critical condition. I called my parents and asked them to come to the hospital to be with me. I also called my ex-husband, whom I'll refer to as Mark, to let him know what was going on. My parents arrived at the hospital within minutes, and Mark and his parents arrived shortly after my parents. At this point, a social worker was asked to come speak with me. She asked if I wanted a cup of coffee or tea, and she said she was trying to make me comfortable because it was going to be a long day. We all were taken to a more private waiting area. My dad proceeded to call our pastor, Rev. Miller, and asked him to come be with us at the hospital. When my pastor arrived, I remember him saying, "Let's pray." We all stood and gathered in a circle holding hands, and Pastor Miller began to pray. I remember hearing my pastor pray and ask God for a miracle, and I suddenly felt my legs go weak, so I quickly sat down in a chair. As my pastor continued to pray, I saw the emergency room doctor quietly enter the waiting room. He sat down patiently, waiting for the praying to stop. As my pastor concluded the prayer, I remember hearing him say, "These blessings we asked in Jesus's name, amen." I looked up and looked directly in the face of the emergency room doctor. I heard no sound: I heard no voice. I remember reading the doctor's lips as he said to me, "I'm sorry, he's gone!" My son had died. It was a few minutes past twelve o'clock at noon, and my son Michael had died from complications of meningitis. The tears flowed down my cheeks, one tear at a time.

I remember my mom embracing me with a tight hug, and as we held each other close, we cried endlessly. I don't remember where my dad was, but I do remember all three of my brothers crying as well. Someone said that one of my brothers threw a chair across the room, and another brother punched the wall. The news of my son's death affected us all tremendously. Words can't explain the emotions that filled that room the moment we were told that my son had died.

Mark had stepped out of the waiting room and was not there when we received the news of Michael's death. His friends had gone to look for him. They stood in front of the elevator, and as the doors of the elevator opened, there stood Mark. They told him that Michael had just died, and Mark took one step out of the elevator and fell to his knees and began to cry. This news was devastating to us all. The sounds of people crying could be heard throughout the entire unit of the hospital. Even the nurses were crying.

I had just gone through my first divorce and was now forced to deal with the death of my six-year-old son. After talking with the doctors and trying to get answers as to what happened with Michael, I was allowed to see him. When I walked into the hospital room and saw my child lying in that bed, not breathing, I became weak and severely lightheaded. I was told that I fainted.

As my family and I were leaving the hospital, Mark approached me, grabbed both of my hand, looked directly in my eyes, and said he was so sorry about our son dying. He continued to say that if there was anything he could do for me, to please let him know. He wanted me to know that he was willing to put aside our differences and be there for me no matter what.

For days, weeks, and even months, I walked around numb. Every day I would cry almost to the point of becoming sick. I knew no other way to deal with my son's death.

I couldn't understand why this had happen. He was healthy, not even a simple common cold. How did this disease take my son's life in less than twenty-four hours? The only way I knew how to handle this was to cry. The doctor told me that he had been practicing medicine for over twenty-eight years and had never seen a case of meningitis as severe as this one, or a case of meningitis that claimed a life as quickly as this case.

There were newspaper articles and news reports on the television about my son. Things were being said through the media that really hurt. The principal at my son's school had called and told me that a child psychiatrist was brought into the school to try to help Michael's classmates understand death and what had happen to my son. I was also told that because meningitis is very contagious, everybody in the school, children and adults, had been advised to see their doctor and to take antibiotics. Although my son died on Monday, he was in school on Friday, which could possibly mean that some people could have been exposed.

A news reporter showed up at the school a day before my son's funeral and randomly interviewed parents, grandparents, teachers, and faculty members. One question asked was how parents were feeling about the meningitis scare. One person said that they could not believe that I sent my child to school sick and risked the lives of so many other people. As I sat and listened to this news report, tears ran down my cheeks. I had just lost my son, and now I'm being accused of being insensitive by sending my son to school sick. Well, my son's teacher came to my rescue. She told the same reporter that Michael was not sick at all on his last day at school. He did not display any signs or symptoms of being sick in any way, not even a sign or symptoms of having a common cold. He didn't cough or sneeze the entire day. He didn't have a runny nose at all that day. He had no fever at all that day. He was just like all the other children at school that day. The teacher proceeded to say that as his mother, I had every right to send him to school. She continued saying that Michael's death was a shock to everyone. "Michael was as healthy as all of us last Friday, and now, tomorrow, his parents have to bury him."

It had been about a week since I had to bury my son. I had been crying nonstop. I just couldn't seem to pull myself together. I wasn't hungry, so I didn't eat. I wasn't sleepy, so I didn't sleep. I remember lying in bed in a somewhat fetal position, crying. My middle brother, Donnell, came into the room where I was and tried to console me. Nothing he did worked. I just laid there and cried. Donnell called my mother because he said he was seriously worried about me. My mother left her job and came home immediately to be with me. I remember my mom sitting on the side of the bed rubbing my back and telling me that everything was going to be all right. God makes no mistakes. My mom kept telling me that I was going to get through this.

She said that we all have suffered a great loss, but we have got to be strong and believe that God is going to bring us through this. I believe my mom was praying the entire time she sat on the side of my bed. I could hear her telling me to be strong, but I know deep inside she was praying. My mom told me that I had to pull myself together for my other children. She said, "Your boys need you. You are going to make yourself sick not eating, not sleeping, and crying all the time. You can't be a good mother to your boys like this. You have got to be strong, pull yourself together, and be the mother your children need you to be for them."

I knew she was right, but I felt that if I could just lay in that bed and cry, all the pain would go away. I continued to cry, and my mom never left my side. She stayed with me throughout the rest of that day.

As the days rolled by, I found myself not crying as much, and I noticed that the pain of losing my son was no longer so greatly intense. I was staying with my parents after my son's death because I could not bring myself to go back to the apartment that I lived in with my son. I went straight to my parents' house from the hospital the day my son died mostly because I did not want to be alone and also because I was not ready to see Michael's room and his belongings.

My mom had returned to work, and she would call me every day to check on me. Some days, I cried; other days, we laughed together. I know my mom loves me. She told me that she didn't know how it felt to lose a child, but she would be there for me no matter what.

It took years for me to get over my son's death. Every year I cried on his birthday, and I cried even more every Memorial Day holiday. At the age of five, Michael had the opportunity to attend Vacation Bible School, at which time he learned the song "Yes, Jesus Loves Me." Michael would sing that song every day faithfully until the day he died. After his death, whenever I heard that song on the radio, in church, or during any musical event, I cried; but eventually, I was able to find comfort while listening to that song, knowing that Michael is in a better place resting with our Lord and Savior Jesus Christ. As time passed, my grieving and the pain I felt became easier to deal with. It was during my time of mourning when I met husband number 2.

In Loving Memory of "Michael" 1986 - 1993

A New Beginning

Months went by, and it was time for me to return to work after my son's death. It was my first day back, and as I sat at my desk working, my coworkers were stopping by to offer their condolences. I believe I cried the entire day. Every time someone came over to my desk to offer a hug, condolences, or even kind words, I cried. It was a tough day, and I needed to find some sort of a distraction, anything that would help keep my mind off my son's death. I asked one of my co-workers to stop people from coming to my desk because I couldn't take any more. I appreciated their kindness, but it was just a little too much for me emotionally. I didn't think I would last the entire day, but to my surprise, I made it through my first day back at work. It was just about time to go home when I heard a deep, strong, sexy voice say, "Welcome back." I looked up and standing next to my desk was a tall, handsome, dark-skinned young man. He introduced himself to me and proceeded to tell me that he was transferred to my department while I was out of work. He continued saying that he was sorry to hear about my son. He offered his condolences, and I didn't cry: I actually had a smile on my face.

From that day forward, every day, this young man would walk by my desk and say hello. Eventually, he asked me out on a date. I accepted, gave him my phone number, and waited patiently for him to call. When he called, we talked on the phone for hours and then made plans to go out. Approximately two years following that initial phone conversation, Adam and I were married. I felt I had found Mr. Right. He was kind, funny, smart, hard working, and most importantly, God-fearing. He was a man that went out of his way to make me feel special.

After we became married, things seem to be fine. Although our marriage had its ups and downs, we had bumpy roads to cross and a few adjustments that we had to get use to, but to me, this was normal: it's what marriage is. Our union wasn't perfect, but I felt in my heart that we were going to be fine.

Not only did I just become a wife, I also became a stepmother. My husband had two children from a previous marriage, who visited us often. During their visits with us, I noticed a lot of mean treatment toward my son Jamel, and I also noticed some jealousy. There would be times when the girls would refuse to play with Jamel; they didn't want to sit next to him at dinner, while watching TV, and even in the car during family trips. They would sneak and hit him when no one was looking, or should I say they thought no one was looking. I was no different than any parent; I stood up for my son and did what I had to do to protect him from the mistreatment and mental cruelty that took place when the girls came to visit. Robert was much older and had no interest in the stepsiblings.

We were no different than any other family; we had good days as well as bad. But I tried everything within my power to make the girls feel loved and comfortable when they were in our home. With my children and my husband's children, we all had become one big blended family.

Three years into our marriage, my husband Adam introduced me to his third daughter. This child was supposedly from a high school crush. She was twelve years old and the eldest of his three daughters. Now I have another stepdaughter, one more person to add to our lovely, big blended family.

After seven years of marriage, I became pregnant with the twins. I thought this was God's way of telling me that everything was going to be all right with my marriage. Two months into the pregnancy, I began to hemorrhage and was placed on bed rest. The doctor told me that I was in danger of having a miscarriage, so I needed to be on complete bed rest. This was just the beginning of my pregnancy problems. At twenty-six weeks, I went into premature labor. I remember lying down for a nap, and when I woke up, I felt contractions—strong contractions. I monitored and timed my contractions for approximately thirty minutes and noticed that every ten minutes, I was having contractions, and they were getting stronger. I called my doctor, and he told me to meet him at the hospital. Upon arriving at the hospital, I was hooked up to the contraction monitor and the baby monitor. After approximately one hour of monitoring my contractions and monitoring the babies' heartbeats, I was admitted to the hospital. The doctor said that they had to get the contractions to stop because the babies would not survive if they were born at this stage of my pregnancy. Days rolled by and then weeks and I was still in the hospital. My contractions had slowed down, but they did not stop. I stayed in the hospital close to the end of my pregnancy.

Finally, I was released from the hospital in late April. The doctor was still keeping a close watch on me. I was in the doctor's office twice a week monitoring my contractions and my blood glucose levels. My twins were born mid-May, approximately two weeks after the doctor released me from the hospital. I gave birth seven weeks early to two healthy little boys, a blessing indeed.

Anthony's Surgery

At the age of five months old, Anthony became sick with what was to me just a common cold. I was at work when I received a call from my sitter saying that Anthony was sneezing, had a runny nose, and a slight fever. I called the doctor and was told to bring him into the office. I left work, went to the sitters to get Anthony, and headed off to the doctor. We didn't wait long before the doctor was able to see us. After a thorough examination, the doctor said I was right, Anthony had what is known as the common cold as well as an ear infection.

Because all babies are born with an underdeveloped immune system, the doctor was reluctant to advise me to give Anthony an over-the-counter medicine.

He explained that our immune system is a complex system capable of amazing things. Its basic task is to protect you by recognizing anything that gets into your body, determining if it is foreign, figuring out if it is friend or foe, and respond accordingly. When our body is faced with defending itself from intruders such as bacteria or viruses, many types of cells within our body spring into action. Some respond by producing infection-fighting proteins called antibodies. Others, such as white blood cells, are able to attack bacteria directly and destroy them. This is how our body's immune system is often able to prevent us from getting sick and helps us get well again if we do become sick. Children are more sensitive to medications than adults. Children are more prone to medication toxicity than adults. If given the wrong dose, some over-the-counter medicines can be ineffective and/or harmful. He also explained that ear infections are usually caused by bacteria and a virus. Ear infections happen when fluid builds up in the area behind the eardrum and then becomes infected. Any fluid that enters the area leaves through the Eustachian tube, which connects the middle ear to the back of the nose and throat. But if the Eustachian tube is blocked, which can happen during colds, sinus infections, and allergy season, it traps the fluid in the middle ear. Germs grow in dark, warm, and wet places; so a fluid-filled middle ear becomes the breeding place. If an ear infection becomes worst, inflammation in the eardrum will cause pain. Fever may develop as well. The doctor told me that Anthony had an acute otitis media. I returned Anthony back to the sitter. Just as I returned to work, I clocked in and received another call from my sitter. This time, it's Andre. He had the same symptoms as Anthony. There was the runny nose and a slight fever. I called the doctor and was told to bring Andre in. Again I had to leave work. I got Andre from the sitter and headed back to the doctor's office. When I arrived, the receptionist said to me, "Weren't you just here a few minutes ago?" and we both laughed. I walked into the examination room, and the doctor thoroughly examined Andre and told me the exact same thing he said about Anthony. Andre had a common cold and an ear infection. Andre's ear infection was in just one ear, whereas Anthony had a double ear infection. Although Andre only had an infection in one ear, the doctor still gave me a prescription for an antibiotic for him and said to give him acetaminophen or ibuprofen for the fever. I had to give the boys the antibiotics for ten days, and the doctor needed to see them for a follow-up appointment to make sure the ear infections had cleared up. Before leaving his office, the doctor said to me, "From now on, when one of the boys become sick, just bring them both in together. The odds are, because they are twins and share a lot of things, when one gets sick, the other will become sick as well. Might as well kill two birds with one stone and bring them in together." This time, when I left the doctor's office, I didn't bother to go back to work. I just picked up Anthony from the sitter and went home.

Although I was satisfied upon leaving the doctor's office, I felt I wanted to do a little research of my own. I wanted to know if it was medically accurate not to treat a five-month-old child with a common cold. I needed to know if this was normal medical practice. I received a prescription for the ear infection but nothing for the cold. I did find out that most doctors prescribe an antibiotic for an acute otitis media in addition to acetaminophen or ibuprofen for pain related to the infection. Some doctors my advice parents to give over-the-counter medicines for the common cold, but others remain reluctant. I guess I was okay with the advice and information given to me by the doctor and the information I found during my research.

My aunt Annie, my mom's sister, was my sitter, so I was able to bring the boys back to her the next day so that I wouldn't have to miss days from work while the boys were sick.

Within two weeks, the boys were doing better. But Anthony still had the runny nose. Three weeks had gone by since the boy had become sick, and Anthony's nose was still runny. My aunt told me that I needed to take him back to the doctor. This is not normal. No one has a runny nose for three weeks straight without something being wrong. So I called the doctor and took Anthony back in. The doctor told me that Anthony had developed another ear infection. He prescribed another antibiotic and told me to make a follow-up appointment for two weeks. Two weeks had gone by, and I took Anthony back to the doctor for his follow-up appointment. Anthony still had a runny nose. This time, I was very interested in hearing what the doctor had to say. During his examination, the doctor told me that Anthony had severe fluid in his ears, and his ears were still infected. Not only did Anthony still have a runny nose, but also, I noticed that he was having a hard time breathing. I noticed that his breathing was becoming more difficult during naps and overnight while he was asleep. We had a baby monitor in the twin's bedroom that allowed us to not only hear the boys, but we could see them as well. I would lay awake in my bed listening to Anthony struggle to breathe during the night. He would snore really loud and then occasionally I would hear him choking. I constantly went into his room to check on him, and I would try to suction as much mucus as I could from his nose. For weeks, Anthony lived with a cotton cloth diaper to wipe his runny nose and a baby bulb syringe to suction his nose throughout the day. Anthony was now eight months old, still had a runny nose, and now has his third ear infection. The doctor was persistent to try to get rid of Anthony's ear infection by giving me another prescription for an antibiotic.

I was not satisfied, in fact, I agreed with my aunt. No one, not an infant, toddler, or adult, has a runny nose this long. Something other than an ear infection is wrong. I demanded that this pediatrician do something other than write another prescription. Because of the fluid on Anthony's ears, the doctor recommended that we take Anthony to an ENT, an ear, nose, and throat specialist. He gave me the name and number of a doctor to call. The very next day, I called to make an appointment. Unfortunately, the appointment was four weeks from the date I called.

Anthony is now nine months old, and we are finally able to see the ENT. During the appointment, the doctor did a thorough examination of Anthony. He told Adam and I that Anthony's ear was indeed infected and that there was severe fluid in his eardrums. He also said that Anthony's tonsils were huge. This could explain the snoring and choking. He also noticed that Anthony's adenoids were large, but before he could make a final diagnosis, he wanted to schedule Anthony for a CAT scan.

I had questions. I needed to know more about what was going on with Anthony. The doctor began to explain that children with large tonsils experience mouth breathing and choking. A child may snore very loudly and may not breathe well while asleep and may actually stop breathing for several seconds. If severe and not treated, this could put a strain on the heart and lungs. He also said that the nose may be blocked by enlarged adenoids, which could cause a child not to smell properly and have a congested nose. Many people know where the tonsils are located, but not everyone knows where the adenoids are located. He proceeded to say that the adenoids are located behind the nose and above the back of the throat. Enlarged tonsils and adenoids usually block a child's breathing passages, also known as airway obstruction. Listening to the doctor, I felt like he had been in my house and listened to Anthony while he struggled to breath. This doctor was explaining exactly what had been happening to Anthony. I told myself that I was not going to panic. I would wait until we get the results of Anthony's scan before I panic.

The day had arrived for Anthony's CAT scan. The ENT doctor suggested that Anthony be placed under anesthesia to help him sleep. Because Anthony was only ten months old, the doctor felt he would not lay still during the scan and in order to receive an effective scan results, it was best to have Anthony sleep during the procedure. We arrived to the hospital, and everyone was really nice to us. They allowed us to get Anthony ready for the procedure, and they also allowed me to hold his hand as he was given the anesthesia. The anesthesiologist warned me that Anthony would become completely limp once the anesthesia was administered. I had no idea what to expect, but as Anthony's little body became limp, it scared me tremendously. He was lying on the exam table looking completely lifeless. My eyes filled with tears as the nurse ask me to let go of Anthony's hand. When I let go, his hand fell to the side of the table as if Anthony had just died. I was completely frightened. Adam grabbed me by the hand and reassured me that Anthony would be all right. We walked to the waiting area together and sat patiently. The entire procedure took approximately twenty minutes, and we were able to go to the recovery room to be with Anthony. He had to stay in recovery for a few hours. The doctor wanted to make sure Anthony would be okay once the anesthesia wore off. The side effects associated with anesthesia were aspiration, difficulty swallowing, coughing, or gagging to name a few. The doctor wanted to wake Anthony and make sure he could swallow without any complications, and of course, his vitals were monitored closely. I was able to sit in a rocking chair and hold him while we waited in the recovery room. The doctor told us that the procedure was a success, and the results should be in his office within a few days. He advised me to make an appointment so that we could discuss the scan results and discuss what would happen next.

At the next appointment with the ENT, he informed us that Anthony adenoids were excessively large, and he wanted to remove them as soon as possible. So he scheduled Anthony for a tonsillectomy and an adenoidectomy as well as inserting tubes in his ears. The doctor explained that placing tubes in the ears drains the fluid and ventilates the middle ear, and it should prevent future buildup of fluid in the middle ear and should decrease the feeling of pressure in the ears, which reduces pain. Tubes normally remain in the ears for six to twelve months. They often fall out on their own, but if they don't, surgery may be needed to remove them. He explained that ear tubes are plastic and shaped like a hollow spool and that the tubes are placed through a small surgical opening made in the eardrum. The doctor felt that doing all three procedures at once was the best solution for Anthony. Adam and I agreed, and Anthony's surgery was scheduled.

Anthony is now eleven months old. It's surgery day. We arrived at the hospital, and again, everyone was really nice to us. They allowed us to help get Anthony ready for his surgery. This time, I refuse to be there as the anesthesiologist gave the medication to help put Anthony to sleep. I stayed in the waiting area while Adam went to be with Anthony. Within seconds, Adam was walking toward me in the waiting area. He said it was quick and exactly the same as the CAT scan procedure. Again he reassured me that Anthony would be fine. We waited patiently for the surgery to be over. An hour and twenty minutes later, the doctor approached us and said that surgery went well. He said that Anthony's adenoids were larger than he thought, but he successfully removed them and he should be fine. He also told us that Anthony may experience a runny nose for a few weeks longer, but once healing takes place, he should be fine. Once the tubes fall out, Anthony should no longer get ear infections. Adam shook the doctor's hand and said, "Thank you for everything." I smiled and said "thank you" as well. We then went to the recovery room to be with Anthony. The nurse told me that she would be waking Anthony in a few minutes, then I could hold him until he is discharged.

I sat and thought about the various medications, needles and surgeries that were involved in my boy's lives. I could only image the levels of mercury my boys endured during my pregnancy, during the surgery, within the prescription medications, and within the vaccinations given. Looking back on these various incidents, I truly believe there has to be some kind of link to autism. Scientist, doctors, and various studies, however, still deny any connection between needles, vaccinations, and medications with autism.

Anthony's surgery was a success. Within one month, his nose stopped running, he stopped snoring, and he no longer struggle to breathe while asleep.

Anthony began to walk at twelve months old while Andre didn't walk until he was fourteen months old. My twins were developing just like any other child their age except they weren't talking. They were crawling at five and six months, they could pull themselves up and stand without assistance, they played with toys, and they watched children programs on the television just as any other child their age. Anthony had the prettiest smile for a little boy. Everyone loved to see him smile.

And Andre had the prettiest eyes. Both boys loved to dance. Anytime music was played, they would dance. My boys had unique qualities about them, just as any other child their age. I couldn't image at fifteen months old that something was wrong, especially autism.

The Truth Hurts

O ne day, my youngest brother, Lonnell, stopped by our house for a visit. We talked, laughed, and joked around for a while. Anthony and Andre were sitting close by in their toddler rocking chairs watching *Sesame Street* on the television. Just before my brother got ready to leave, he went over to play with the boys. As he was leaving, he asked me if the boys were okay, and I replied yes. I wasn't exactly sure what my brother was getting at and why he was asking if they were okay, but as far as I was concerned, my boys were fine.

Approximately two days later, my mom called and said that my youngest brother was concerned about my twins. He felt that something was not right. My twins are now sixteen months old and could not talk. Lonnell thought that this was strange. We have a big family, and all the children in our family at least said *mommy* and/or *daddy* at fifteen months or earlier. But not my twins. They don't talk at all. I was kind of offended by my brother's accusations. Although my brother was just showing concern, I was still offended. Nothing is wrong with my boys, and how dare he even suggest such a thing.

A few days later, I thought about what my brother had said. I realized that as a parent, you don't want anything to be wrong with your children, and most parents would be quick not to accept that something could really be wrong. It was time for the boys' eighteenth-month doctor visit. During this visit, I was given a form to fill out regarding my boys' progress. One of the questions on this form asked if my child(ren) could talk, say one or two words, or just babble. I didn't check either box because my boys didn't talk, say one or two words, nor did they babble. Once in the examination room with the doctor, the doctor saw that I had not checked anything regarding the boys' speech ability. I told him that none of the choices applied to be boys. He continued with the examination. Just before leaving the examination room, I asked for his opinion as to why my children weren't talking yet. He said that Anthony had so much fluid in his ears, everything he heard sounded like being underwater. This could explain why Anthony couldn't talk. Now that he has the tubes, and once they fall out, Anthony will be able to hear and should start talking. I accepted that explanation for Anthony, but what about Andre? He didn't have tubes inserted into his eardrums, so why doesn't Andre talk? The doctor told me that most twins feed off each other. Once Anthony starts talking, then Andre should follow.

The boys were growing fine. Their height and weight was fine. The measurement of their head circumference was fine. They would make eye contact. Their reflexes were fine. Everything about Anthony and Andre was fine. The only thing that troubled me was the fact that my boys could not talk. There was an occasional babble, but there were no words.

We had a follow-up appointment with the ENT doctor to check the status of Anthony's tonsils, adenoids, and ears. Everything was fine except the tubes had attached themselves to Anthony's eardrums so surgery had to be schedule to remove them.

Anthony is now twenty-two months old. The tubes had been successfully surgically removed. He was doing great. No more snoring, no runny nose, no more ear infections, yet he still could not talk. He and Andre both.

I refuse to give up on finding the answer to why my twins could not talk. Not only were they not talking, they were not potty trained, they were no longer making eye contact, they did not play with other children, and I noticed a big difference behaviorally between them and other children their age; they also showed no interest in coloring, writing, or anything academic-related. I voiced my concerns again to the pediatrician, and just before the boys turned three, the pediatrician recommended that they be tested for autism.

My Family's Support

My boys are getting older, taller, and much stronger, which makes handling them a lot harder on me. I have three brothers that really look out for me. When I lived in New York and my boys were first diagnosed with autism, my brothers really stepped in and helped me in every possible way. If Anthony happens to have a meltdown and my brothers were close by, they would always come to my rescue. One Sunday, while in church, Anthony had a severe temper tantrum. My mom tried to help me with him, but we both were unsuccessful. My brother Burnell Jr. and my brother Donnell saw my mom and I wrestling with Anthony, and they immediately took over. They saw that my mom and I were getting nowhere with Anthony. On that particular day, handling Anthony was a challenge for them as well. After wrestling with Anthony for about ten minutes, they eventually had to carry Anthony to my car because he was totally out of control. People were standing around, watching and whispering, and I just wanted to cry. Once they were able to get Anthony into the car, he was still in an uncontrollable rage. Anthony twisted, turned, and kicked so much till it caused my parked car to rock from side to side. My brothers stayed with Anthony until he calmed down completely. I am so grateful to my brothers because they never hesitated to help no matter what.

My brother Donnell, I would say, is God-sent; he is my hero. He knew that life had become overwhelming for me. Although he worked many hours on his job, he would regularly come and get my boys and take them to birthday parties or just let them hang out with his daughter at the park or sometimes hangout at Chuck E. Cheese. My brother knew that my boys would not interact with his daughter or other children, but he would still come and take them for a few hours. He said he just simply wanted to give me a break.

My son Jamel is now a teenager and was involved in the performing arts. He has performed in several plays, musicals, and talent shows. I try to support him as much as I can. I don't want Jamel to think that I only have time for the twins. I do whatever it takes to divide myself and my time between my children. I may not be able to divide myself equally, but I try to make sure that each child receives a portion of my time no matter what.

Not only was Jamel involved in the performing arts, but he also was involved in sports. Jamel played basketball, softball, and football. I tried to involve myself as much as I could in all activities Jamel became involved in, not only the performing arts but sports as well. I remember a relative telling me to take the twins to Jamel's football game and let them run around in the open space. This relative told me that letting the twins run around would tire them out, and once we got home, the twins would pass out sleep from exhaustion and should sleep the entire night. The only problem with that theory is allowing the boys to run free would totally exhaust me physically and mentally. There is two of them and only one of me. The odds that they would run together were slim to none. They would end up running in two different directions, leaving me to decide who to chase first to reassure their safety. Realistically, there was no way I could watch Jamel play football and keep up with the twins all at the same time. I try to support my children equally, but because there is only one of me, it's almost always impossible.

My youngest brother, Lonnell, would babysit the twins so that I could support Jamel and attend most of his performances and games.

Now that I have moved to Maryland, I don't have that family support that my brothers gave while we were in New York. People often ask me if I consider moving back to New York, and I constantly say no. I like living in Maryland, and I have to believe that things will work out for my boys and I here in the state of Maryland.

I had a friend once tell me that I am not the only woman on this earth to become divorce and have to raise children alone. When I approached her to talk, my intentions were not to imply that I have been singled out in this world. I know that there are thousands of women that are divorced and raising children alone. I guess I was just looking for an outlet, someone to just listen to me. All I was trying to convey is that I really feel that parenting is harder for women than for men, especially single parenting. And parenting is even harder when the child has a disability. As I talked to this friend, I tried to tell her that this is not the life I once dreamed of for myself. I was trying to share with her that I never thought I'd be divorced twice, a single parent, and nevertheless, raising children, twins with a disability. I began to cry as I was talking to my friend. Because it doesn't take much for me to cry, I was labeled and definitely I feel that I was misunderstood during the entire conversation.

I don't believe that people should be quick to pass judgment when they have never experienced life as I know it. A person that has never lost a child should not try to tell someone else how to deal with it. I've often heard the words "'Going there' cannot tell 'been there' how to get there," but people do it all the time. Because I am a very emotional person, I know that I am very much misunderstood and often judged.

I do know that there are other women in this world that have similar life issue like mine, if not worse. Being told not to stress is easier said than done. When you feel like the rug of life has been snatched from up under you and you have to fight harder than the next person to survive, stress is the first thing you grab hold to.

By the time my twins turned four years old, I was into extensive research, hoping to find something that would give me hope as far as a cure for autism. I was searching basically for anything that could help me help my children. As a child, I had always dreamed of becoming a nurse. With all the information and knowledge I had gained during my autism research, I figured this would be the perfect opportunity to go back to school and become a nurse. I could better educate myself regarding the medical aspect of this disability called autism.

The Big Move

There I was, a single parent working full-time, attending school part-time, caring for autistic twins, and trying to keep up with my now teenage son Jamel and his sports. I was running from school to school, appointments to appointments, trying to keep up with my housework. I had to prepare daily meals, help Jamel with his homework, do my own homework, and somehow find some time for myself, which rarely happened. By the end of each day, I would literally pass out from complete exhaustion.

There had to be an easier way of life. I refused to believe this is how life was going to be for me. I needed a change, so I began to entertain the ideal of leaving New York State and starting a new life and creating a new beginning for myself. This was indeed a scary thought but by far the best ideal I had had in years, so I began to put this ideal into action. My first step started with researching different states. The first thing I needed to know was how each state handled education for children with autism and which states had the biggest need for nurses. I researched the states of Texas, North Carolina, California, and Michigan. I was impressed with North Carolina when it came to nursing jobs, but North Carolina did not have the education for autism

I was seeking for my boys. In fact, none of the states I researched had the academics in autism that I wanted for my boys.

One day, while at work, a co-worker gave me a flier regarding the nursing shortage in the state of Maryland. Maryland was not an option, so I wasn't interested in the information that was given to me. But just for fun, I did a little research on Maryland. To my surprise, I found that Maryland, Howard County had an outstanding report card score. The academic program for autism was very interesting; it had indeed caught my attention. Also, I found that Maryland had a huge shortage of nurses. The more I researched about Maryland, the more impressed I became. Having family in Maryland helped me gain more accurate information regarding education, cost of living, and nursing jobs. I then packed my bags and made a trip to Maryland. I visited a couple of schools and hospitals in the different Maryland areas. I was so impressed with what was said to me and the information I gathered, I added Maryland to my relocate list; actually I made Maryland state number one on my relocation list. After months of contemplating, it was time to make a decision. But before I could make a final decision, I wanted to visit Maryland one more time. During this visit to Maryland, I visited different places to live, such as apartments and condos.

It wasn't long thereafter when I decided to give the state of Maryland a try. Maryland was my ultimate choice. I packed my bags and relocated to the state of Maryland.

My move to Maryland would be the first time I had ever been away from my parents and my brothers. This was a huge step for me. I was scared, and I was not completely sure it was the right thing to do nor was I sure this move was actually going to work. I knew I would probably get homesick and want to move back to New York, but I was determined to push my fears aside and give Maryland a try.

A week after my move to Maryland, I really began to miss my family. I had to talk myself into believing that everything was going to be all right. As I thought about it, I realized that it took a lot financially and physically to move to Maryland, so I needed to tough it out and stay.

I had a meeting with the school board officials the Monday after moving to Maryland. They wanted to discuss where to place the boys. They needed to know what levels the boys were currently at. Andre had begun to say a few words but could not form a complete sentence. He also was partially potty trained. He would still have a lot of potty training accidents, but he knew how to use the potty and not wet on himself as long as we were home. Anthony was still not potty trained and was still completely nonverbal. The meeting with the school officials lasted well over two hours. They wanted to make sure both boys would receive the services they needed and that they were placed in the school that could help them the most. I was completely impressed and happy with the educational system in Howard County, Maryland. I appreciated the school officials taking the time to make sure my boys were placed in the right schools and that they would receive the special services they needed. I felt as though these school officials really cared.

It's been a month after our move and Anthony was still having the potty training accidents that kept me mopping and cleaning up poop. I did not have a support system in Maryland like I had in New York. I was pretty much alone. I do have family in Maryland, but it's not like the family support I had in New York.

Andre was much more advanced than Anthony. Andre had learned how to be independent since he started school in Maryland. Whatever he learned in school he was proud to try at home. Andre took great pride in being independent and doing things on his own; for instance, he really likes pouring juice into a cup.

After dinner one night, Andre went back into the kitchen, opened the refrigerator door, grabbed the carton of juice, and tried to pour the juice into his cup. He spilled almost the entire carton of juice all over the kitchen counter, the kitchen floor, on the carpet in the dinning area, and on himself. By the time I got into the kitchen, he had made a huge mess. I cleaned him up and then cleaned up the rest of the mess that he had made. As soon as I finished cleaning the kitchen, I could smell that Anthony had had a potty accident. As I walked into their bedroom, I stepped on poop. There was poop on the floor, on the footboard of the bed, in both of Anthony's hands, in his hair, and on the bottom of his feet. I spent most of the night on my hands and knees cleaning up juice and poop. The tears begin to flow down my cheeks, one tear at a time.

I thought, this stage of autism was over. I moved to Maryland for a new beginning but soon realized that there is no new beginning with autism.

Life had become extremely overwhelming for me. With all the responsibilities I endured on a daily basis, my nights were filled with exhaustion. We had just finished eating dinner, and I sent the boys into their room to play while I cleaned up the kitchen area. After washing dishes, sweeping the floor and wiping off the kitchen table and countertops, I decided to sit down for a few minutes to rest. From where I was seated, I could watch the boys every move. I was so tired I accidentally fell asleep. When I woke up, I could smell Anthony. I just grabbed my bucket, cleaning towel, and cleaning products and headed straight for his room. Just as I expected, it was as if Anthony had finger painted the room with poop. By the time I got Anthony out of the tub and cleaned up his potty accident, it was late, and I was tired. My eyes were blood red from crying. It was a proven fact that I could not leave the boys unsupervised, not even for sixty seconds. Therefore, simple tasks such as using the bathroom while the boys were awake were done in fear. I had become afraid that leaving them alone to use the bathroom would have unfavorable results. My household chores had to be done while the boys were asleep. Let's face it, I am a single parent with no help whatsoever. I basically cater to my boys 95 percent of the time, which meant very little or no time for me. There had to be more to life than just caring for my children and cleaning house.

About a year after moving to Maryland, my youngest brother, Lonnell, came to visit me. He actually said he was thinking about moving to Maryland. Nevertheless, I really enjoyed having him around. It was nice being with family and having help with my boys.

Early one morning, as I got up to get ready for the day, I was in for an unwelcomed surprise. Just like any other morning, I walked into the kitchen to fix breakfast, I would then proceed to get everything ready to dress the boys and get them ready and off to school. Now it was time to wake up the boys and get this day started. I walked into the twins' bedroom, stood in the doorway and screamed. Lonnell came running to see what was wrong. While I was in the kitchen cooking breakfast, Anthony had awaken and while lying in the bed, ripped his pull-up into shreds. Andre looked like he had been in a snowstorm. Both boys were covered in cotton. As my brother approached the room and looked in, he immediately knew why I screamed. I began to cry. He told me not to worry. My brother said to me, "Get the boys and yourself dressed, I will clean up this mess." He told me that he didn't want me to be late, plus he came to Maryland to help and that's what he was going to do. I know my family loves me. They have always shown true love toward me, but I've see their love even more since my boys have been diagnosed with autism. My brother said it took him over forty-five minutes to completely clean up the wet cotton mess that Anthony had made.

I have been told that I complain, whine, and cry a lot over my life situations. Maybe I do, but through my tears, I'm not looking for sympathy or a pity party. I blame myself totally for how my life has turned out. I often say that if I had made different or better life decisions, I'm sure my life today would be different and definitely better. But at the same time, if I turn to a family member or a friend, I'm not looking for a solution or critism, I'm simply looking for a shoulder to lean on. My life as it is, is very complicated, and most times I'm just looking for a temporary escape.

Finding a Church

I was starting to feel frustrated again. I needed an outlet. I needed to do something other than care for my boys.

Church—I needed to find a church to attend. I needed some spiritual encouragement, and going to church would give me just what I needed. Because I was new in town, I had no idea where to start looking for a church, so I surfed the Internet looking for churches in the area that I could possibly visit. I found a few churches, wrote down the addresses, and set out to visit each one. I ended up all over the Maryland area. I visited churches in Columbia, Baltimore, Hanover, and even a church in Washington, DC. I found myself at a Baptist church, an AME church, a Church of God, and even a nondenominational church. There were big churches, and some were very small. The denomination and size didn't matter to me; I was just looking for spiritual encouragement.

Anthony and Andre do not handle crowds very well, and they have a hard time sitting for more than thirty minutes at a time. Most church, Sunday morning services would last approximately one hour or longer, which would pose a problem for my boys.

As we entered each church, we were pleasantly greeted by the ushers and escorted to our seats. Once seated and the service had begun, I was amazed at how the people treated us. After thirty minutes of sitting, Anthony would become frustrated and began to display his frustration verbally and physically. Of course I was embarrassed, and I tried everything within me to quiet him down and keep him calm. Most time, I had no success. The remarks and looks that we got were very hurtful to me. People would stare at my boys and some people even got up and moved their seat. I know that my boys can be disruptive and the tantrums that Anthony would display were an even bigger distraction, but it really hurt my heart to sit and watch people actually get up and move away from us. News flash, autism is not contagious.

I can image how people felt. I didn't like how my boys behaved either during church services, but at the same time, I did my best to keep them calm and quiet. No matter what, some people still looked at us and treated us like we had the plague. I'm sure those that looked down on us had no clue that I was dealing with autism times two. They had no clue what was actually happening with my boys. All the churches we visited, no one ever stopped to ask if they could help nor did they try to find out why my boys were acting out. People would just automatically acknowledge my boys' behavior as misbehaving, not disability-related. We were guilty without trail.

There were times when I had to leave a Sunday service early because Anthony would become really frustrated, and I was afraid that he would have one of his uncontrollable tantrums. Every church we went to, people treated us like outcast. I became frustrated and seriously discouraged, so I stopped visiting church services all together.

One Sunday, while visiting a certain church, Anthony had an accident that made me not want to go out in public with the boys any more, ever again. I was excited about attending church this particular morning. I was still learning my way around Maryland and was proud of myself for finding this church without having to be shown the way and without getting lost. When we arrived, the service had already begun. I sat down and tried to enjoy the singing. Just as the singing ended and the pastor got up to speak, Anthony got up and sat in my lap. I didn't want him to spaze out on me, so I let him stay seated in my lap. About ten minutes into sitting on my lap, I felt water running down my legs. I made Anthony stand up, only to notice a puddle in my lap. Anthony had wet through his pull-up into the lap of my skirt. I didn't know what to do. Should I stand up, stay seated, or what? As the puddle left my lap, I noticed it had formed on the floor under my feet. I just grabbed Anthony and had him to sit back in my lap. I was so embarrassed. I figured that if Anthony was sitting in my lap, no one could see the wet spot on my skirt or the wet spot on Anthony's pants. As we continued to sit in a puddle of urine, my nose suddenly became consumed with a urine odor. I know the young lady sitting next to me saw everything. When I made Anthony stand up, she looked at my lap at the same time I did. Here I sit in the pew of this church, wet and starting to smell. I can't do this, I need to leave. I grabbed my purse and told the boys, "Let's go." As I left the sanctuary, I told the usher what had happened and I apologized. As I was walking down the steps of the church, the usher called out to me as she held up a set of keys. She asked if left my keys. I looked at the keys and realize that they were mine. I left in such a hurry that I left my keys on the pew. As I got to my car, I noticed that not only was the front of my skirt wet, but the back of my skirt was wet as well. I was so embarrassed. I can image how many people saw that wet spot on my skirt as I left the church, and I sure can imagine what they thought, and most of all, what they must have said.

One Saturday, a friend of mine from New York whom I'll call Roxanne, who was attending grad school in DC, called me and invited me to come to the church she was attending. She explained that there was going to be a guest speaker that she felt I would really enjoy. I hesitated with my response. After what we had been through with all the churches we visited, I wasn't too thrilled about visiting another church. I didn't want to subject my children and myself to the funny looks and unruly treatment people offered as I exhaustingly dealt with autism. I explained to Roxanne how I felt. I asked her how large the congregation was because I'd rather not go or try to find a sitter instead of subjecting my boys to rude and nonunderstanding people. She proceeded to tell me that she would help me with the boys. She promised me that I wouldn't be alone. I begin to seriously consider her invitation, but at the same time, I was still hesitant because I just did not want to be bothered with the unfriendliness from yet more church people. I really wanted to go, but I felt in my heart that I would not enjoy the service, and the people would not accept my boys and this thing called autism.

Roxanne was persistent in trying to get me to change my mind. I told her that I would think about it and call her back with my decision. After that phone conversation, I couldn't get my mind off wanting to go to church. I really needed to be in a church service. I longed for spiritual encouragement.

I took my chances and called a young lady whom I'll refer to as Beatrice, who works at the daycare center my boys attended. I asked her if she would be available to watch the boys for me while I attended a church service. I did not expect a positive response because it was a last-minute request. To my surprise, Beatrice said yes. I was so excited I immediately called Roxanne and told her that I would meet her at church. Roxanne and I agreed on a time to meet at church and hung up. I was so happy, actually I was so excited that I would be able to attend a church service and would be able to go without the boys. I was actually going to get a break from the boys and enjoy myself all at the same time.

On Sunday morning I got up, fixed breakfast for the boys, cleaned up the kitchen, and got the boys settled for the morning. I then begin to get myself dressed for church. Beatrice arrived on time. I gave her instructions on caring for the boys and proceeded to leave for church. I knew it was going to be about a twenty-five–minute drive, so I left the house with plenty of time, ensuring that I could drive safely and accurately follow my directions to this church. I made it. I had arrived at the *Refreshing Spring Church of God in Christ*, located in Riverdale, Maryland. I looked around the parking lot and did not see Roxanne, so I called her from my cell phone. She told me that she was running a little late, but she should arrive within ten minutes. So I parked my car and sat in the parking lot waiting for Roxanne to arrive. Just as she said, she pulled into the church parking lot exactly ten minutes later. We both got out of our cars and embraced each other with a hug. We walked into the church and sat down. I couldn't help but notice how beautiful the sanctuary was. I started to think how things would be if I had brought the boys. This place is big and nice-looking. The people here probably would treat my boys just like all the other churches we had visited. I had to shake these negative thoughts. I came to this church looking for spiritual encouragement, not for negativity. To my surprise, I enjoyed the service tremendously, and the guest speaker was fantastic! I enjoyed myself so much that I was looking forward to coming back to visit again. Everything I felt I needed spiritually I got from that service. I sang, I clapped my hands, I worshipped, I cried, I heard encouraging words, and I most of all enjoyed the praise. I couldn't wait to come back and visit again.

The week was over, and Sunday was approaching fast. All I could think about was going back to the Refreshing Spring Church of God in Christ to visit again. I still was not ready to take the boys with me to this church, so what am I going to do? I decided to try my luck again and call Beatrice. Once again, at the last minute, I wanted her to watch the boys for me, and again she agreed. Two weeks in a row, I get to attend a church service without the boys. This never happens to me. I'm starting to feel like everything is going to be all right. Things are going to work out for the boys and me.

Again, I enjoyed the church service. I told Roxanne I really like this church, and I think I would like to join, I wanted to become a member, but I was afraid that things would not work out for my boys. She told me that she wanted me to meet the pastor, Rev. Dr. James E. Jordan Jr. Every Sunday, immediately following each service, the pastor and his wife would stand at the exit and greet the people as they proceeded to leave the church. Roxanne walked in front of me as she walked toward the pastor. She said that she was going to introduce me to Pastor Jordan and let him know that I was interested in joining the church.

With this introduction, the pastor shook my hand, and I begin to tell him that I had really enjoyed the services, and I was interested in becoming a member. I proceeded to tell him about my boys. I explained to the pastor that I have twin sons who are both autistic, and I needed to be in a church environment that would be understanding and compassionate to their disability. I told him how we had been treated at other churches that we visited, and I was afraid of the same thing happening at this church. Pastor Jordan told me to bring my boys to church with me, and he guaranteed me that I would experience nothing less than compassion and love at this church.

As I continued to talk, the pastor began to look around and called for a young lady that helps out with the youth church. I later found out that this lady also works as an elementary school teacher in the Maryland state area. He introduced us and began to tell her that I wanted to join the church and that I have twin boys who are both autistic. This lady was so nice to me. She begin to explain the youth church to me and she told me that when I bring the boys to church, that I should look for her and she would help walk me through the youth church procedures and help me with getting my boys involved.

Just as I got ready to walk out of the church, I looked up and saw a poster on the back wall that said, "Love one another."

The following Sunday, I returned to this church, this time with my boys. I again enjoyed the service. It seems as though my boys enjoyed the service as well. I saw both Anthony and Andre clapping their hands and smiling as if they too were enjoying the service. The next Sunday, I became a member of the Refreshing Spring Church of God in Christ.

April is autism awareness month. During the month of March, I had the opportunity to speak directly to Pastor Jordan regarding autism and asked what could be done to educate the congregation about autism. The pastor asked me to bring him information such as pamphlets, brochures, literature, etc., whatever I could get regarding autism. He asked me to also give him a photo of my boys. I had no clue as to why the pastor had asked me for all this information and I had no clue as to what he was going to do with all this information.

It was the first Sunday in April, and as usual, when we walked through the church doors, we were greeted by an usher and were handed a church program. As I sat in my seat, I began to read through the church program and was delightfully surprised to see that there was a small article regarding autism. As the pastor addressed the congregation, he asked everyone to pay attention to the article about autism. He urged the members to educate themselves about it. I begin to smile as he told the congregation not to be quick to judge without properly educating themselves regarding this disability. My smile became even bigger as he proceeded to talk about Anthony and Andre.

The last Sunday in April, I walked into the sanctuary again greeted by an usher and reached for the weekly program. I looked at the front cover and my face immediately lit up! There on the front cover of the program was a big picture of Anthony and Andre. Inside the program was another article regarding autism, and right next to the autism article was a brief bio about Anthony and Andre. As the pastor stood at the podium, he asked me to bring the boys to the front of the church. He wanted the entire congregation to meet the two little boys whose picture appeared on the front cover of each program. My heart was beating very fast. I was nervous, but yet, I was overwhelmed with joy. I had only been a member of this church for four months, but it didn't matter. The compassion and love that Pastor showed toward my boys and educating the people about autism really touched my heart. It showed that he really cared. To date, I am in love with my church family. As the pastor promised, my boys and I have been shown much love and compassion since we joined. I knew that I had joined the right church family. I got just what I was looking for at this church: spiritual inspiration, spiritual guidance, and a lot of brotherly love. I knew in my heart this was home. We belonged here, here with a church family that knows how to show love no matter what.

Now that I am a member at the Refreshing Spring COGIC, I have become very comfortable with having the boys in church with me. Anthony and Andre have different stimulation needs. Anthony uses a string and Andre a pencil for stimulation. Anthony loves to twirl his string and lash it out like a whip at different objects. One Sunday, while in church, Anthony was twirling his string and whipped it right into the neck of a young man sitting in front of us. All I could see was this young man's shoulders go up, and he turned around to see what hit him. I couldn't apologize enough. He said it was okay, but I can image what was really going through this young man's mind.

One Sunday, while trying to calm Anthony down, standing in the lobby area, a church mother came to me and said that I should stop apologizing to people because my sons are disabled. She told me that she also raised a special-needs child, and she too had to learn to stop apologizing for his disability. She said that she watched me deal with my boys in church, and she thinks I'm doing a great job with them. People don't understand how difficult it is to raise a special-needs child, but that's no reason to apologize.

I went back into the sanctuary and was able to stay until the service ended. As we were walking out of the church, Anthony, although he is nonverbal, was very loud with the sounds that he makes, and I insisted on making him be quiet. A young lady sitting on the back pew said to me, "Let him speak the way he knows how. One day, we all are going to be able to understand what he is trying to say." Her words brought a smile to my face, and I had no choice but to agree with her. I continued to smile as I thought to myself, people do truly understand what I'm going through and that the church mother was absolutely right; I need to stop apologizing.

It's Called Progress

Within four months of living in Maryland and attending school in the Howard County school district, Andre had become completely potty trained, and he is able to formulate a full sentence. Andre had become very independent. He is able to dress and undress himself, open and close doors, lock and unlock doors, and he can verbally tell me what he wants without having to use pictures or hand gestures. He has improved tremendously.

Andre has extensive sensory needs. He often carries a pencil with him for self-stimulating behavior. He is found twirling pencils between his fingers constantly. He requires movement, such as a swing or circular sit-and-spin. Back rubs have been found to be a good reinforcer to promote positive behaviors. He enjoys watching DVDs and interactive computer websites and games. His love for DVDs displays his repetitive behavior. Andre will rewind a DVD over and over again until he can repeat the entire movie verbatim. He is also very proficient on the computer. He has a photographic memory, which has helped him with his reading and math. Andre is a very smart little boy and has made tremendous progress since our move to Maryland. Andre currently receives speech and occupational therapy in school. I have been told that Andre could be more advanced academically, verbally, and socially if he were receiving additional services such as speech and occupational therapy at home.

Anthony is still nonverbal and still not potty trained. However, he is doing great with sign language and using pictures to communicate. Anthony on occasions still has the tantrum meltdowns, and because of this, the school has added a behavior specialist to his weekly IEP services. He has an infatuation with strings. He can be found twirling a string nonstop on a daily basis. The occupational therapist has said that this is a form of stimulation; it's actually a big sensory need for him. Not only will he twirl a string, but he will twirl any objects that resemble a string, such as a man's necktie. Some reinforcers that have been found to be good for Anthony are just about anything physical such as squeezes, spinning him, picking him up, and twirling him, hands rubbed with lotion, bouncing on a ball, and scooter rides. Anthony loves to swing, climb, jump, and flip. He loves the trampoline and jumping in his bed. He currently uses a voice device machine to help him communicate on a daily basis both at school and at home.

It has been said that my twins are super smart. For a child with autism, education and special services should not just be limited to school but needs to be implemented at home as well. Being a single parent with limited financial resources, there's only so much a mother can do. I live a busy life, but I always make time to do what I can for my children, and somehow it never seems to be enough.

My first trip back home to New York after moving to Maryland was for Thanksgiving. When we walked into my parents' house, Andre looked at my mom and dad and said hello. My parents were overwhelmed with how well Andre could talk. They were excited that Andre remembered them and could address them individually. They were excited at how well he articulated his words.

While at home, I was watching the Oprah Winfrey show, and the topic that day just so happen to be about autism. One of the guests on Oprah's show that day was Mrs. Holly Robinson-Peete. Holly has a son that has autism as well, so she knows about the world that I live in. The only difference between me and Holly is that she has a husband to share life's pressures with, and she only has one child with autism. I am single by way of divorce, and I'm raising two children, twins, with autism.

I was very impressed with the passion that Holly displays toward autism. I read Holly's story in a magazine while standing in the checkout line at Walmart. From reading this article, I knew that Holly was scheduled to appear again on the Oprah show to speak about autism. I wrote to the Oprah show asking for a chance to meet Mrs. Holly Robinson-Peete. I knew that millions of people write to the show, trying to be a guest, but I thought I'd try my luck. Because of her passion for autism, I just wanted the opportunity to meet Mrs. Holly Robinson-Peete and speak with her, hoping that she could share information that could help with my daily journey with autism. I believed in my heart that through her words and her advice, I could have received a small piece of inspiration and encouragement and maybe would have gained a piece of knowledge of something different I could do to help my boys.

I received a return e-mail from the Oprah show coordinators telling me that they received my request but could not give any guarantees that I would be invited to the show due to the numerous amounts of requests they receive daily. Unfortunately, I was not one of the lucky ones invited to the Oprah show. But it's okay. Yes, it would have been nice to meet and talk with a celebrity that is dealing with similar issues, but it didn't happen. So I will just continue to do what I know as my best for my boys.

Anthony is the twin that is very affectionate. He loves to hug and kiss on the cheek. He has a smile that can brighten up any room. A lot a people fall in love with Anthony because of his affectionate side alone. When he's not in one of his violent rages, Anthony is very adorable and very lovable. My twins are very close. As infants, they were so little that we let them sleep in the same crib for months. One night, while checking on my babies, I noticed that they were holding hands. I thought that was so cute. I called Adam into their room because I wanted him to see how cute the boys looked sleeping and holding hands. To date, they sleep in the same bed. I tried twin beds, but it didn't work. Every morning, either Anthony would get out of his bed and get in bed with Andre, or Andre would get in Anthony's bed. Either way, they were put to bed in separate beds but woke up the next morning in the same bed. So I eventually traded the twin beds for one full-size bed, and now the boys sleep every night comfortably together in one bed.

Andre is very protective of Anthony. He will not let another child do anything to Anthony that may cause harm. Although Andre is the youngest of the two boys, he's the biggest and tallest, and he assumes the role of the big brother. Anthony is more laid back and would rather give and receive affection versus being protective.

Andre is also a kid that thrives on routine. He likes things done as planned and always in order. God knows I hate when school is closed due to inclement weather. I have the hardest time explaining to Andre that there is no school due to bad weather. One particular day, it had snowed, and schools were closed. Although schools are closed, I still have to go to work so the boys stay at the daycare center for the day. On days like this, I have to get Andre to understand that there is no school. As we approach the door, every morning we gather in a huddle and pray before we leave the house. After we pray, Andre would grab his book bag. I tried to tell him that he didn't need his book bag because there was no school. He replied, "Yes, Mommy, I am going to school. I will see my teacher." I again tried to explain to him that schools were closed because of the snow. I reached for his book bag, and he became very upset and started to yell. As I have mentioned, my boys are older, taller, and much stronger. Andre held on to that book bag with all his strength. We played the tug-of-war game for a few seconds, and I just gave up. I allowed him to take his book bag to the daycare center. As we arrived to the daycare center, Andre began to yell again. A daily routine for Andre is to ride to the daycare center in my car, get out of the car, stand at the bus stop, which is located in front of the daycare center, and wait for the bus. I got out of the car and told Andre that he had to go inside the daycare center because schools are closed. He began to yell, "I have school, I will see my teachers." I grabbed his hand and told him to walk into the daycare center because there is no school. He refused to go into the daycare. He actually pulled against me because he did not want to go into the daycare center. At this point, I have lost my patience with him, so I began to yell. I grabbed Andre by his cheeks and looked him directly in the eyes and told him that he would be in trouble with me if he didn't start walking toward the daycare center *now*! He still refused. I grabbed him by the hood of his coat and literally dragged him into the daycare center. The entire time, Andre was yelling at the top of his lungs and pulling against me, which made the whole ordeal just that much harder. I had become extremely frustrated and upset. It took several minutes to get him inside the daycare. Once I got him into the daycare center, I explained to the workers why Andre was so upset. They already know that he has autism. They told me to leave and go to work, not to worry, and that they would work with him. One particular daycare worker told me that she would get Andre to understand that school was closed for the day.

I took advantage of the ride to work to calm myself. I work at a hospital in the labor and delivery unit. Being frustrated and upset with my child was not the right attitude to take to my job.

People often watch me deal with my twins and compliment me on a job well done. Being a single parent raising twins with autism can be a very difficult job. Every day I give my all to make sure my boys have what they need as they live with this disability. I have often been told that my boys are blessed to have me as their mother. But I have to admit, there have been times when I felt like I was going to lose control. I have never thought about abusing my children, but I have been pushed to limits that have made me seriously frustrated and upset.

One day, as I sat and watched the news on television, I became interested in a story about a young lady that was babysitting a ten-month-old child. She said the child started crying and wouldn't stop. So she picked up the child and shook the child, threw the child on the sofa, and the child stopped crying. Not only did the child stop crying, the child also stopped breathing. When she realized the child had stopped breathing, she ran for help, but unfortunately, this child died and this young lady went to jail. This child had died from Shaken Baby Syndrome. As I sat and listened to this story, I felt really bad for this young lady because I understand how children can frustrate you and cause you to have a reaction that you can and will regret. I don't agree with her reaction of shaking the child, but I truly understand and know how a child can push you to extremely high levels of frustration.

I often receive compliments stating that I am a good mother, but to me, I'm just like any other mother that loves her children. Just as any mother, I have my days when my patients and frustration levels are challenged.

The only difference between me and other women is that most women don't have twins with a disability.

I can remember a day when my patience had been truly challenged. The boys and I had attended Sunday morning church service. Everything was fine until minutes before the benediction. Anthony had a mini outburst just as church was about to end.

Church service was over; we left the building and got into the car. As I was driving home, Anthony became severely outraged. He usually sits right behind me in the rear seat of the car. He leaned up and grabbed the collar of my coat. He had such a strong grip on my collar, almost to the point of choking me. I tried with all my strength to relieve Anthony's fingers from my collar while at the same time trying to drive without crashing. I started thinking to myself, *What is wrong with this boy? He is going to cause me to have an accident.* It never dawn on me to pull over, I just began to drive faster because I needed to get off the road before I crash my car and possibly hurt all of us. I was able to pry Anthony's fingers off my collar, but then he started screaming, yelling, and kicking the back of my seat. I continued to drive as fast as I could, praying that I wouldn't get a speeding ticket. I had become completely overwhelmed.

I made it home. Anthony got out of the car, fell to the ground kicking, screaming, and crying. I picked him up off the ground. He stood on both feet for about two seconds and then came at me as if he was trying to bite me. I was starting to lose my patience. I grabbed Anthony by the coat and literally dragged him toward our apartment. Upon entering the hallway of our apartment, Anthony once again tried to bite me. I pulled him toward me and told him to stop the madness. I then redirected him to walk toward the door of our apartment, and he resisted against me. At this point and time, I no longer had any patience with Anthony. I grabbed his arm and pulled him toward the stairs. Suddenly I lost my balance and fell down the stairs. Because I was holding on to Anthony, he too fell down the stairs. I became furious. As I realized that I was okay, I reached for my keys, unlocked the door, and pushed Anthony inside the apartment. I snatched his hat off his head, grabbed the front of his coat, unzipped it, and noticed that Anthony's nose was bleeding. Anthony had stopped crying and wiped his nose with his hand. I rushed him into the bathroom so that I could care for him. As we headed toward the bathroom, he touched the walls and grabbed the doorknob. There was a trail of blood from the front door to the bathroom. There was blood on the floor, walls, doorknob, and the bathroom sink was saturated with blood. I wanted to cry. I could not believe this was happening. I'm not sure when Anthony's nose began to bleed. Did it happen during our fall or while I wrestled with him to get him into the house? Within minutes, I was able to stop the bleeding. I cleaned Anthony up and then cleaned up the rest of the house wherever there was blood.

After cleaning up, I sat alone quietly in my living room thinking about what had just happened. I love my boys very much and would never do anything to harm them. I couldn't help but wonder if raising my boys alone was becoming too much for me. The tears began to flow, one tear at a time.

Support Groups

Since I moved to Maryland, I have met a few mothers of children with autism. Our children were all attending the same school at this time. I truly admired and envy these women. I envy them because they have husbands that help them daily and they get breaks that I only dream of. There is one young lady that is recently divorced, but her ex-husband is very active in their son's life, which also gives her that same break that I can only dream of. I found these ladies to be wise, educated, smart, and very supportive toward me in every way possible.

We all usually get together once a month for what we call girls' night out. It's a night away from home and a break away from autism, mostly a night out at a restaurant enjoying girl talk, dinner, and no kids. During girls' night out, we also share autism stories and share information about resources that are available to help our children. We talk about the education that our children are receiving, and we discuss progress, if any, that our children have made. Many times, I am not able to attend girls' night out because I don't have a sitter. The other girls are able to leave their children at home with their husbands. Because I'm single, I must find a sitter, which becomes another financial issue for me. Being single with one income in my household and having two children with autism makes attending girls' night out a little more difficult for me. These ladies are married with a two-income household and only one child with autism; I can't compete with that. No matter what, I feel like I always lose. But in order to make it possible for me to attend girls' night out, these ladies would be willing to allow me to host girls' night out in my home. Although the purpose behind girls' night out is to get away from home, these ladies understand my situation, and they have no problem making an exception on my behalf. Also, a couple of the girls in the group have reached out and contacted different resources in an attempt to help me find a dedicated, permanent sitter—a sitter that will be dedicated to helping me with my boys. I couldn't have asked for a better group of friends.

There are days when my boys and I spend quality time together and have lots of fun. During the winter months, snowy weather usually means school closings. I take advantage of these days to spend quality time with my boys. One particular winter day in the state of Maryland, schools had been closed for two days. Even though schools were closed, it's still business as usual in my house. I still have to fix breakfast and then clean the kitchen afterward. After eating breakfast, the boys both would come into my room and climb into my bed, and we would all watch television together. After a few minutes of watching television, I would read to the boys. I would drill the boys with flash cards, testing their knowledge with the alphabet, numbers, colors, and different words. Then we would sing and play various games together. We sometime would play the tickle game. This seemed to be the boys' favorite. I would tickle the boys, and they would try to tickle me. The laughter shared during our quality time warms my heart. It reassures me that our bond is strong, and I feel that I have done well as their mother.

I would like to get my boys into different activities and/or sport. I thought about basketball for Andre because he is so tall, and gymnastics for Anthony because he loves to climb, jump, and flip. I also thought about signing the boys up for Cub Scouts. After reading the Cub Scout brochures that were sent home from school, I often considered signing my boys up to join. According to the brochure, my boys have all of the qualifications to become a Cub Scout, except an active father. I could attend Cub Scout meetings with my boys but one of the main ideas of a Cub Scout is father-and-son time. I have registered my boys with the Big Brother, Big Sister program, hoping to find a man that wouldn't mind spending time with my boys and attending Cub Scout meetings with them. I think my twins could learn a lot as Cub Scouts and the experience would be great for them. Plus, I know that they would look cute in those little Cub Scout uniforms.

My plate is full enough these days, but I still long to get my boys involved in some sort of sport activity. I really feel it would be good for them and being active in sports could also help them socially. I want so much for my boys, but I'm only one person. There's not enough of me to go around, and there's not enough hours in a day to do what I would like for them.

In order to keep my boys active and convince myself that I am keeping my boys active socially, I purchased a toddler basketball rim and a toddler T-ball game. During our quality time, we play basketball and T-ball. I challenge the boys to see who can make the most baskets or who can hit the baseball the farthest. Although Anthony is nonverbal, every time he hits the baseball off the T-ball stand, he holds both arms up in the air as though he's claiming victory and then he raises his hand petitioning me to give him a high five. Both Andre and I clap and praise Anthony for a job well done. Anthony also enjoys putting the basketball into the hoop. Andre shows more interest in basketball than he does baseball. Andre also likes to play catch with a kickball, another toy I purchased for them. Watching my boys interact with the toys reassures me that they are making progress. I know that getting them involved in athletic activities outside of the home would be good for them also. It's okay to interact together, but they also need to interact with other children as well.

Springtime in Maryland usually brings about nice weather. During the spring and the summer, I usually take the boys to the park. Anthony loves to swing, but most of all, he loves to climb and swing from bar to bar on the jungle gym. Sometime he makes me nervous the way he swings from those bars. But as I watch him, he seems to know when there is danger. I consider Anthony my little daredevil. There is not much that he won't try. Things that I feel are dangerous, Anthony goes out of his way to conquer. There have been times when my heart is pounding with fear. I am so afraid that Anthony is going to fall and hurt himself, but to date, he has not had any accidents whatsoever. He just simply enjoys himself every time.

Andre loves to run. At the park, he may swing for a few minutes, but then he takes off running. There is a bike trail at the park, and this is where Andre goes to run—the bike trail. It's hard keeping up with the boys. I want to keep an eye on Anthony because I'm afraid he's going to fall and hurt himself, and at the same time, I need to watch Andre because I'm afraid he may run out of the park to a place that is out of my sight. I need to be able to see him at all times. I do carefully split my attention between the boys. I constantly talk to Andre, allowing him to hear my voice. I tell him to stay where I can see him while at the same time, keeping my eyes on Anthony. Both boys really enjoy the park. We usually stay about one hour and a few minutes and then go home.

I also take the boys swimming during the summer. We always have fun swimming. I cannot swim and this makes me nervous at time about having the boys in the water. Therefore, I won't allow the boys to go any deeper than two feet in the pool. One particular day at the pool, Andre and I were splashing each other with water, laughing and having a good time. While in the pool, I am very careful to make sure that I can see both boys at all time. It's been a few minutes, and I have seen nor heard Anthony. I began looking around for him. I stopped playing with Andre, so I could look for Anthony. I didn't want to start worrying, but I didn't see Anthony. Just as I started to walk through the water,

Anthony floated right by Andre and I. I could not believe what I was seeing. Anthony had taught himself to swim. I was amazed! I could not believe this. Because I can't swim, I had to assume that Anthony taught himself to swim. This was amazing to me. Although Anthony is nonverbal, he has other characteristics about himself that shine very bright and stand out strong. I think Andre takes after me. He doesn't know how to swim either, so we end up enjoying swim time by splashing each other while Anthony enjoys swim time by actually swimming.

I try to keep the boys involved in as many activities as time will allow. The more active they are, the easier it is on me. Anthony doesn't have tantrums when he's doing things that he enjoys, like climbing the jungle gym and swimming. Keeping my boys busy with different activities really makes my life a little easier. I may be exhausted by the end of the day, but I'll take exhaustion any day over dealing with uncontrollable tantrums.

Andre's ability to communicate has improved tremendously, and I think I often underestimate his abilities. Andre is a very smart kid, and he is catching on very fast. I often find myself still placing Andre at the level he was at when we first moved to Maryland. Months ago, if you asked Andre a question, he would not answer you; he would just repeat the question. Now Andre is able to answer almost any and all questions that he is asked. One day, I asked him where he wanted to go for his birthday. He told me Chuck E. Cheese. I assumed Andre had just seen a Chuck E. Cheese commercial on TV and didn't really understand the question I had just asked him. This particular birthday, I took the boys to the park to let them play. I had bought cupcakes and ice cream and had planned to celebrate their birthday with just the three of us. I had convinced myself that the boys really didn't understand the concept of birthday parties, so I didn't bother to plan one. As we got in the car to leave for the park, Andre asked me, "Mommy, are we going to Chuck E. Cheese?" I was shocked. I truly thought Andre had seen a Chuck E. Cheese commercial. I did not think that Andre understood the concept of a birthday party. Still not sure that Andre completely understands, I responded yes. As I began to drive home, Andre started crying and telling me that I was driving the wrong way. He pointed out the window and said, "Chuck E. Cheese is that way." I was blown away. He actually understood the question I had asked him, and he actually knew the correct way to get to Chuck E. Cheese. I was not prepared financially to take the boys to Chuck E. Cheese or to celebrate their birthday with a party, but because my child was in the back seat of the car crying and saying that he wanted to go to Chuck E. Cheese, I took him to his favorite store, Wal-Mart, and allowed him to buy a DVD of his choice. He was happy. The tears stopped and then I was happy. Andre has progressed tremendously, a lot more than I had thought.

One winter day, it was predicted that we would get eight inches of snow. It was a Saturday morning, and the snow was falling very fast. Andre pulled back the blinds, looked out the window, and said, "Mommy, I love Christmastime." I had the biggest smile on my face. Andre knew that the snow falls during Christmastime. Although Christmas had left, he thought it was coming back because it had started to snow again. About a year ago, Andre knew nothing about snow or Christmastime. It was at this moment I knew that my child had truly made great progress with communication and with comprehension.

Autism Can't Wait

Life with autism is not all bad. Yes, it has its cross to bear, but I don't believe God would give me more than I can handle. I would love to have my children autism-free, but that's not my reality right now. Doctor's and psychologist have said that my boys have autism; I say my boys have life. I am their mother, and I will continue to love and care for my boys as long as they need me. Some days are better than the others, but we have a lot of love for each other and that alone outweighs the bad.

There are many resources such as government funds and private agencies that offer financial help and special services such as speech and occupational therapy for children with disabilities. People often offer me information as to how to apply and receive help through various agencies, and to date, all I've got is being placed on waiting lists. So many children are being diagnosed with autism until funds are not available. The waiting lists are usually one to three years, and as more children are being diagnosed and parents are looking for help, it's now predicted to be up to a five-year wait. From the day my boys were diagnosed with autism, I have been told that the earlier you get help for them, the better.

Starting therapy and receiving special services would increase their chances at living a highly functional life. There is no time to wait when it comes to autism; help is needed now.

I'm Speaking Out

When speaking with other parents, especially single parents that are dealing with autism and similar issues, I tell them that they need to learn how and when to pick their battles. Over the years, I've learned to stop complaining, stop whining, and stop feeling sorry for myself and just simply pick my battles. It's a hard task and a rough journey, but over the course of time, I've learned that the best solution is knowing what to do, when to do, and how to do. I don't have all the answers, nor do I know how to solve it all, but as a parent, I know my children and I recognize their likes and dislikes and the dos and don'ts and from this I've learned how to pick my battles.

Over the course of my journey with autism, I discovered that people are going to stare, laugh, make smart, unkind remarks, and even move away from you like, autism is contagious. But I've learned to smile and ignore as much as I possibly can because not everyone understands or wants to understand. Although the cruel responses from the different people hurt, what works for me is to continue to smile and move forward past all the nonsense.

I visited a website called Autism Apparel online and ordered T-shirts that say, "I have Autism." Whenever we go to places where there is likely to be a crowd, I usually put these T-shirts on my boys, and I've noticed that most people are a lot nicer when they know without having to ask what's different about my boys. I have had a lot of people stop me and say that they know someone with autism. I've had parents stop me and say they have a child that has been diagnosed with autism. The T-shirts usually make people a little nicer and much more compassionate and often people are full of questions. I'm not sure if it's my approachable personality and/or my warm smile, but after reading my boys T-shirts, people would often approach me and ask questions. We were at the mall, and I decided to window shop at a nearby jewelry story. The salesclerk read my boys' T-shirt and started asking me a variety of questions about autism. She went on to tell me that her son was displaying a peculiar behavior that prompted the pediatrician to suggest that he be tested. She went on to tell me that she was very reluctant because she did not believe in her heart that anything was wrong with her son, and most importantly, she did not want her son to be considered disabled and eventually labeled. After talking to this woman for approximately thirty minutes, I believe I was able to convince her to at least seriously think about having her son evaluated. We exchanged telephone numbers, and I told her to feel free to call me any time if she had more concerns and questions.

I don't like a lot of attention especially when it comes to my boys, but I'd rather let the clothing my children wear grab someone's attention especially if it can educate people about autism and if it could help someone that is struggling over the decision to have their child tested or just simply having a hard time dealing with an autism diagnosis.

I know that my twins don't like crowds. When it's time to go shopping, I find a sitter or when I have to take the boys with me, I try to arrive at the mall early. I actually try to arrive when the doors are first opened. This is how we avoid crowds, therefore avoiding meltdowns.

While at the mall with no crowds, the boys have a lot of space to jump, hop, twirl, and or yell without the stares and negative comments. Anthony loves the waterfall at the mall. While at the mall, we cannot leave until we stop by the waterfall where Anthony just stand and stare at the water. One day, Anthony got away from me and started running very fast toward the waterfall. Thank goodness I was able to catch up with him just in time to stop him from jumping into the water. I literally grabbed him by the collar, which stopped his foot from going into the water. Oh, the joys of being alone in the mall with my autistic twins. There is never a dull moment.

Going to the barbershop can be challenging as well. I was lucky enough to find a barber that takes appointments. I usually try to schedule haircut first thing in the morning for the boys. We get up on a Saturday morning, eat breakfast, get dressed, and head off to the barbershop. I've learned that getting out early to get things done is the best solution for us. After a long day of school, church, or any kind of activity, I found that the boys are prone to be more irritated and will become frustrated, which will make things harder for me. So I try to schedule necessary activities during the early morning before their day gets too busy.

The same goes with going out to the movies, dinning out, taking vacations, and attending Sunday morning church services. In the state of Maryland, the Howard County Autism Society often sponsors a special-needs movie day. One of the local movie theaters will reserve a theater for special-needs customers only. They will post signs that will alert everyone that this particular theater is reserved for special needs customers only for the day. I thought this was a great idea. Without this special theater reservation, there is no way I could take my boys to see any movie. The first movie I took my boys to see at this theater was *Alvin and the Chipmunks 2: The Squeakquel.* I was completely fascinated with the atmosphere. There were families there just like our family. There were big sisters and little sisters, big brothers, and little brothers all helping their siblings that have autism. No one got mad when a child yelled out during the movie. No one got mad when a child stood up in his chair and begin to sing very loud. No one got mad when a child ran to the front of the theater and stood directly in front of the screen. As families living with autism, we all knew what to expect, and everyone respected the entire atmosphere. I bought three small bags of popcorn for my twins and myself and enjoyed quality time with my boys out at the movies. I feel this was a great way for the Howard County Autism Society to help parents of special-needs children pick our battles. There is no way I could have taken my boys to a regular movie theater. People would not have been as understanding. I am a member of the Howard County Autism Society, and I often receive e-mails of special events that are taking place in the surrounding community. I try to participate as much as I can with as many activities as I can. My goal is to keep my boys involved while having fun and spending quality time together.

Dining out does not happen often with our family. This is one battle I've learned to just leave alone. I've tried a few times since living in Maryland to take the boys out to a restaurant. We usually end up leaving early, or I may just leave the restaurant, take the boys out to the car, and sit and wait until the rest of my party is ready to leave. Both of the boys are very picky eaters, and most restaurants don't serve what they like to eat. I've even tried feeding them before we go out to a restaurant along with bringing snacks that I know they like. I guess one could say that I'm just trying to figure out ways to keep them calm and entertained so that I could enjoy dining out. Taking my boys out to a restaurant is not too much different than any other child at a restaurant, with or without a disability. Most children are loud, they cry, they don't like the food, they are almost always guaranteed to knock over their drink, and all children always need to use the bathroom right in the middle of dinner. So like any parent, I've learned that if I'm going to enjoy dining out, I need to hire a sitter. Why torture the boys when I know they don't favor dining out. I've learned to pick my battles. The best solution for us all is to hire a sitter.

It has been a while since I have had professional pictures taken of the boys. It's hard to get Anthony to sit still long enough to capture a decent picture. Since the age of three, most pictures of Anthony have no smile, just a blank stare. I want that beautiful smile that Anthony had as an infant and toddler to be captured in his pictures. The blank stare looks so sad. Trying to get Anthony to cooperate with a professional photographer leads to Anthony becoming frustrated, which leads to a possible meltdown. This is another situation where I had to learn to pick my battles. As much as I would like a professional picture, I have to remember that I must pick my battles. I have a personal camera that I use, and most of the time, just as a professional photographer, I am unsuccessful at capturing a decent picture of Anthony.

Andre will sometimes smile. He has heard other children at school saying "cheese" during picture day. So now, when Andre sees a camera, he immediately says, "Say cheese," but unfortunately, there is no smile on his face. I have once or twice been able to capture a smile on Andre's face with my personal camera, but I still long for that professional photo of both boys. I'm hoping that someday, as the boys get older, I will be able to capture again the beautiful smiles of my twins in a professional photo.

Going on vacation is no vacation at all for me. It's always twice as much work for me, especially being away from home. Trying to dress, feed, and entertain the boys while respecting others' property is a huge task. I am so overprotective of my boys. I am afraid that things will happen to upset people, especially those that aren't used to being around my boys. Having a non–potty trained eight-year-old does not usually go well with most people. The accidents that happen at home are not welcomed and usually cause a great deal of anger and frustration to other people. I don't think anyone should have to deal with angry or frustrated relatives or friends while on vacation. Most vacations, I have found myself walking on eggshells, picking up constantly behind my boys, watching their every move, afraid of the comments that may be spoken against my boys. I know what autism is, and I know how it affects most children, but not everyone does nor do they care. It doesn't matter who it is, family or friends, everyone doesn't understand nor are they compassionate toward autism. Because of this, I sometimes become reluctant to take vacations.

I have been accused numerous times of using autism as a crutch. I have been told that I let my boys get away with unruly behavior, and then I blame their behavior on autism. I disagree with this accusation. I believe in my heart that my boys know the difference between right and wrong. As a parent, I do believe in discipline. I do not by any means hide behind their disability. I feel in my heart that my boys will never recover from autism if I just let them run wild with no direction. Andre loves DVD movies and a part of my discipline toward him would be to take away what he loves most (his DVDs) when he's misbehaving. Also as part of my discipline toward the boys, I would make them go to bed early. Most times, all it takes is for me to raise my voice very loudly, and the boys' behaviors change immediately.

Not everyone thinks that I hide behind my children's disability. I have been told that some people actually think that I am doing a great job with my boys. I'm not looking to be judged or criticized; I'm just doing my best to raise my boys into young men.

The journey I've traveled thus far in my life includes being raised in a two-parent family, being a wife, dealing with broken marriages, becoming a single parent, raising twins with a disability, losing a child to death, being a stepmother, being a Christian, being educated, and most of all continuing to be humble, none of these experiences could have ever prepared me for *life with autism.*

No matter how much research I've done, how many doctors I've talked to, no matter how much advise I've been given, and how many years I've had to deal with autism, I will be the first to admit that I have not mastered nor have I conquered this thing called autism. Every day is trial and error. I don't have all the answers, and I probably never will, but I will continue to do what I feel is best for my children. Like any parent, I wasn't given a manual or a booklet of any kind that explains how to raise children especially children with autism. But I love my children, and I do what any parent would do for their children. I will continue to provide my children with shelter, food, clothing, and most important a whole lot of love. Some days I don't feel that it's all enough, but it's all I know to do.

I have found that a percentage of the African American population are reluctant to have their children tested or evaluated for autism or any disability, fearing that their child will be labeled and treated unfairly academically as well as singled out in society. There is a stigma among African Americans that says once labeled disabled, your child can and will be pushed to the side, ignored, mistreated, and left behind. This is why I believe being educated about autism and the benefits available is very important in the African American community, but this needs to be highlighted in all communities so that parents will feel more comfortable about having their children tested and/or evaluated and be able to move forward with getting the help our children need and deserve. Parents need to know the seriousness behind autism. Through proper and accurate education, parents will learn the importance of early diagnoses and learn how to effectively help their children after they have been diagnosed.

Being told that your child has a disability is no great joy. But denying the reality will only hurt your child in the long run.

Many parents will ignore the signs and tell themselves that their child is okay. I know a parent that had become upset because a loved one suggested that they have their child tested. Ignoring the signs or denying that anything could be or may be wrong is the worst thing any parent could do to their child. Taking that first step, admitting something is wrong, is the toughest step. In the beginning, I had my reservations. I kept telling myself that my children would outgrow the signs and symptoms that they displayed, and I also was upset with my brother when he suggested something may be wrong. Because of my denial, I hesitated to move forward and accept reality. Once I allowed myself to let go of denial and accept the reality of my children being disabled, my biggest fear was the financial hardship I imagined I would have to face. Many families don't have the financial resources to properly help their children, but that doesn't justify denying the disability. Some parents have convinced themselves that their child is all right and have decided to live with that decision. What they fail to realize is their choice to live in denial means denying assistance and special services that are available to help their child survive and possibly overcome autism.

Life Goes On

My twins are now eight years old. Although Anthony has made some progress, he is still nonverbal and not potty trained, but Andre, on the other hand, continues to make tremendous progress in every aspect of his life. Through the special services that Anthony receives in school, we have been able to find ways to communicate with Anthony. He uses sign language, pictures, and a voice device as different forms of communication. His teachers have reassured me that the sign language, the pictures, and the voice device is not a replacement as far as Anthony speaking; it's just a temporary form of communication until he actually begins to speak and become completely verbal. Anthony still receives speech therapy regularly in school. Using the voice device gives us hope that Anthony may possibly one day repeat the sounds and words that he hears from the voice device. It's also hopefully that the sound and words that he hears in speech therapy may one day prompt him to verbally repeat what he hears in speech therapy. I have been told that Anthony's therapist has reported that once or twice is has been witnessed that Anthony has repeated words such as *bye*, *string*, *stop*, and *go*.

I often worry more about Anthony because he is nonverbal. I have to be an advocate for Anthony in every aspect of his life. My greatest concern is making sure that Anthony is not being mistreated, neglected, taken advantage of, or abused. He has a voice but cannot speak, so as his parent; I have to be the voice that speaks out on his behalf. My involvement in my twins' lives is very important to me.

Just as I worry about Anthony, I also worry about Andre. My worries for Andre are fewer than those toward Anthony. Andre has advanced tremendously. Andre is now able to help me with Anthony to a certain degree. Andre now is able to tell me that Anthony has had a potty accident, which has stopped the poop accidents and has cut back on the wet cotton incidents. Andre is very neat, organized, and very particular about keeping things clean. He has no problem cleaning up after himself and Anthony. He will also help me clean up around the house. Andre can become frustrated with Anthony at times because Anthony is not as neat as Andre. They remind me of the television show *The Odd Couple*. Andre will, at times, help Anthony get dressed and help Anthony put on his coat and zip up his coat. Andre will help fasten Anthony's seat belt in the car, and Andre will unfasten the seat belt once we have reached our destination. Although he is autistic as well, Andre has become quite the little helper.

Our lives are like thousands of puzzle pieces, some big, some small, some pieces are broken, some not fitting at all. But as their mother who loves them very much, my job is to gather these puzzle pieces and try to put them all together and keep them together the best I know how.

I dream of the day when Anthony will begin to speak. I yet have faith that both my boys will recover from autism and grow up to be great men of this world. I know that doctors and psychiatrists have said that there is no cure for autism, but I believe God. Prayer, faith, and hope is what gets me through each day. People often say that they couldn't walk in my shoes. Well, I'm not sure how I've managed to walk in my shoes thus far. I often wish I didn't have to walk in my shoes, but the reality is these are my shoes and I will continue to wear them, and I will wear them well. I believe that what God has for me it is for me. I may not understand why or like where my life is now, but I know that everything I go through is for God to get the glory.

My journey is long from being over. I acknowledge that we have a long way to go with autism. I continue to do the best I can with my twins academically, emotionally, physically, and financially because I'm in this to win. I still don't get a lot of sleep, and I participate very little in social activities, but to see the slightest progress in my twins make it all worthwhile. Through the good and the bad, and the highs and the lows that comes with raising twins with autism, it all has definitely made me a stronger woman and a greater mother. I don't know what the future holds for me and my boys, but I do know that with God all things are possible.

Endnotes

1   (http://www.en.wikipedia.org/wiki/Autism, 2009)
    (http://www.autismspeaks.org/what-autism/learn-
    signs, 2011)